Non Executive Director
(Best Kept Secret Revealed)

By Ade Asefeso MCIPS MBA

Copyright 2014 by Ade Asefeso MCIPS MBA
All rights reserved.

Second Edition

ISBN-13: 978-1499378924
ISBN-10: 1499378920

Publisher: AA Global Sourcing Ltd
Website: http://www.aaglobalsourcing.com

Table of Contents

Disclaimer 5
Dedication 6
Chapter 1: Introduction 7
Chapter 2: What You Really Need to Know 13
Chapter 3: How to Become a Non Executive Director or Trustee 19
Chapter 4: Key Attributes Organisations Look for in Non Executive Director 27
Chapter 5: Top Issues to Understand Before Accepting Appointments 31
Chapter 6: Becoming Non Executive Director 37
Chapter 7: Using Non Executive Directors to Expand Your Executive Universe 41
Chapter 8: The Role of Non Executive Board Directors Today 45
Chapter 9: Public and Not for Profit Non Executive Director 51
Chapter 10: Start-ups Non Executive Director 55
Chapter 11: Start-ups Guide to Managing Non Executive Directors 59
Chapter 12: Executive and Non Executive Directors Responsibilities by Law 61
Chapter 13: Boards Led by Non Executive Chairmen 67
Chapter 14: Reasons for Appointing a Non Executive Director 75

Chapter 15: The Personal Attributes of Effective Non Executive Directors 81
Chapter 16: Non Executive Directorship Best Kept Secret 85
Chapter 17: UK Corporate Governance Code 87
Chapter 18: Non Executive Director Remuneration 95
Chapter 19: Board Diversity 99
Chapter 20: Diversity the Canadian Way 103
Chapter 21: NHS Non Executive Appointments and Ethnic Diversity 107
Chapter 22: Women at the Top.. 111
Chapter 23: General Perspective on Diversity 119
Chapter 24: Conclusion 123

Disclaimer

This publication is designed to provide competent and reliable information regarding the subject matter covered. However, it is sold with the understanding that the author and publisher are not engaged in rendering professional advice. The authors and publishers specifically disclaim any liability that is incurred from the use or application of contents of this book.

If you purchased this book without a cover you should be aware that this book may have been stolen property and reported as "unsold and destroyed" to the publisher. In this case neither the author nor the publisher has received any payment for this "stripped book."

Dedication

To my family and friends who seems to have been sent here to teach me something about who I am supposed to be. They have nurtured me, challenged me, and even opposed me…. But at every juncture has taught me!

This book is dedicated to my lovely boys, Thomas, Michael and Karl. Teaching them to manage their finance will give them the lives they deserve. They have taught me more about life, presence, and energy management than anything I have done in my life.

Chapter 1: Introduction

Most people have heard the term Non Executive Director without actually knowing what they are, much less what they can potentially do for a start-up or growing business.

But those who are in on the non executive secret know that they can add knowledge, contacts and general been there, done that wisdom to a company's board. All of which cannot fail to be of value to a company whatever its size. Allow us to enlighten you.

In April 2002, the UK Treasury and the Department of Trade and Industry (DTI), concerned to improve the productivity performance of British industry, initiated a review of the role and effectiveness of Non Executive Directors (NEDs) in publicly listed companies in the United Kingdom. The review was motivated by the belief that stronger and more effective corporate boards could improve corporate performance.

Derek Higgs, an investment banker, accepted the invitation of the Chancellor and the Secretary of State for Trade and Industry to undertake this review and to issue a set of recommendations based on his findings.

The Higgs Review of the Role and Effectiveness of Non Executive Directors was published on 20 January 2003 and contained a number of proposals to improve corporate governance and enhance corporate performance, including recommendations for changes to the Combined Code. The Financial Reporting Council (FRC) invited comments on these changes and is currently developing a revised Code taking into account the comments it has received.

The analytical and survey evidence prepared as part of the Higgs Review found that the standard practices by which Non Executive Directors are selected often overlooks talented individuals from a broad variety of backgrounds with the skills and experience required for effective board performance. The Review made several recommendations about how companies might improve the quality and performance of their boards through changes in the ways they identify, recruit, select and train individuals to serve in NED positions.

In addition, the Review proposed the creation of a group of business leaders and others to suggest how companies might draw on broader pools of talent with varied and complementary skills, experiences and perspectives to enhance board effectiveness. The Review recommended that this group pay particular attention to ways to bring "to greater prominence candidates from the non-commercial sector who could have the skills and experience to make an effective contribution to the boards of listed companies. The group will describe the profile of relevant skills and experience that make an effective Non Executive Director with a non-commercial background.

At the invitation of the DTI, Dean Laura D'Andrea Tyson of London Business School agreed to chair such a group. We will refer to the group's findings later in this book.

Enough of history so what is a Non Executive Director?

A Non Executive Director sits on the board of a company alongside the executive directors. They act as an independent voice on every important decision. He or she will not work full time, though, and won't be concerned with day to day issues.

They will have to have a full understanding of the running of the company. This means knowing what each department does and being familiar with monthly sales figures and accounts. This allows them to make informed decisions in the interests of the company.

A Non Executive Director (NED, also NXD) or outside director is a member of the board of directors of a company who does not form part of the executive management team. They are not employees of the company or affiliated with it in any other way and are differentiated from inside directors, who are members of the board who also serve or previously served as executive managers of the company (most often as corporate officers).

Non Executive Directors are sometimes considered the same as an independent director, while other sources distinguish them from independent directors saying Non Executive Directors are allowed to hold shares in the company while independent directors are not.

Non Executive Directors have responsibilities in the following areas, according to the Higgs Report, commissioned by the British government published in 2003.

1. **Strategy:** Non Executive Directors should constructively challenge and contribute to the development of strategy.

2. **Performance:** Non Executive Directors should scrutinise the performance of management in meeting agreed goals

and objectives and monitoring and where necessary removing senior management, and in succession planning.

3. **Risk:** Non Executive Directors should satisfy themselves that financial information is accurate and that financial controls and systems of risk management are robust and defensible.
4. **People:** Non Executive Directors are responsible for determining appropriate levels of remuneration of executive directors and have a prime role in appointing and where necessary removing senior management, and in succession planning.

NEDs should also provide independent views on:
- Resources
- Appointments
- Standards of conduct

Non Executive Directors are the custodians of the governance process. They are not involved in the day-to-day running of business but monitor the executive activity and contribute to the development of strategy.

In the UK in 2011 the Financial Times launched the first formal qualification specifically for Non-Execs. The Non Executive Directors Certificate is a level 7 master's postgraduate qualification accredited by Edexcel.

There is a distinction between the role of a non exec in a larger company and one in a start up or smaller one.

As with any contract, there will be arranged working hours. In larger businesses, this time will be spent in board meetings. But start-ups often need someone who is willing to roll up their sleeves and get involved on the days they are in the office. There is time for this because board meetings won't tend to be such long formal affairs. But with bigger companies, the board meeting part will take up a much longer time and the non executive will not be required to deal with specific issues.

Pros and Cons

Pros
1. They are outsiders and you should be able to rely on them to be objective.
2. They should be able to balance the need for short term profit and long term results.
3. Minimising crises should come more naturally as they have probably seen it all before.

Cons
1. Experienced non execs may be tempted to interfere where they are not needed.
2. You may feel a non exec is superfluous in a company that runs well without one.
3. Even if fees are small, there is a risk that non execs may not pay for themselves.

Chapter 2: What You Really Need to Know

It can be all risk no reward! When being approached for a role as Non Executive Director of a major company. Indeed, why risk tarnishing a so-far impeccable business career by being on the board of a company where you share all the responsibility, yet have limited information and insight into the running of the business? However, the lure of being a Non Executive Director remains attractive to many and, despite the perceived risks, a considerable number of successful executives take on Non Executive roles, some going on to build portfolio careers where they sit on a broad range of businesses and organisations.

The reasons often stated for taking on a Non Executive Director role are varied and change throughout an individual's career. For many current Executive Directors, it is to gain new perspectives and insights, learning about another sector and understanding a different organisation's approach to threats and opportunities. Others state that being a Non Executive Director helps them to understand their own board better and enables them to appreciate their perspective to decision taking. Indeed, many up-and-coming executives are often encouraged by their Chairman to seek out Non Executive Director opportunities where they will gain valuable insights and enhance their boardroom skills, developing themselves to be better equipped executives in their current company.

Being a Non Executive Director meant different things to me at different times. My first Non Executive role was during my mid 40's; I was a CEO and I was interested in acquiring different experience and positioning myself in a different place. I found this experience to be highly valuable when running my own show, recognising different ways and approaches and I learnt how to balance views and not be too dogmatic.

For others, perhaps nearing retirement or who have recently stepped down from full time executive roles, the shift of focus tends to be on giving something back, imparting experience to younger management teams and adding value to a company. It is also a means for some to maintain their interest in business; to gain new experience and perspectives. Being a Non Executive Director can also provide an element of identity and a certain stature within social circles, in addition to maintaining intellectual activity and involvement.

Why be a Non Executive Director?

The relative flexibility of being a Non Executive Director can also present an attractive alternative to a busy executive career, enabling experienced executives to create a more balanced lifestyle to suit their personal needs and desires. Often they have created enough wealth to be comfortable with and seek an alternative to the sometimes highly pressurised, all-consuming nature that executive careers can often be in today's 24x7 global economy.

Being a Non Executive Director can be tremendously rewarding and experienced Non Executive Directors often comment that being associated with success and feeling that they have made a difference are key motivators for them. They enjoy seeing a company progress and evolve and know that they have played a part in this success, perhaps by steering a proposal through the Board and witnessing its successful delivery. When you see a company thrive, being able to point to things that you know you contributed to, but the Executives own, is hugely rewarding. However, being a Non Executive Director requires considerable influencing skills and not all advice will fall on fertile ground.

Those who were former CEOs especially, comment that not being in charge and getting their own way can be tremendously frustrating at first, and can take some adapting to. Non Executive Directors also mention that they can occasionally feel like an outsider, never really feeling part of the team, and that they miss the daily interaction and cut and thrust of business. Others cite frustrations including late Board papers, the "ever-increasing" corporate governance and the feeling that you are "sometimes only there to tick boxes". The Chairman is responsible for setting the tone of the Board and frustrations mount when there is a weak Chairman who doesn't encourage debate, is disorganised and focuses on the "wrong" things rather than tackling the key issues facing the company.

When it does go wrong, it can go spectacularly wrong. When a company is in crisis, the time you will need to commit to sort out the problems can increase dramatically. And with increased media attention on Board governance, once "invisible" Non Executive Directors are often put in the spotlight and can be vilified for "being asleep on the job", "lacking attention to detail", and "being the puppets of an all-powerful CEO". It is often flattering to be approached and asked to join a board. For some however, it can be a time-consuming role for little reward and, for an unlucky few, successful reputations has been tarnished.

The real measure of a Non Executive comes during a crisis when tough decisions need to be made.

Whatever your reasons for taking on your first Non Executive Director role, the opportunity can be fulfilling, stimulating and fun. You need to be conscious that as a Non Executive, your reputation is your currency in the market.

The generic attributes organisations typically look for from their Non Executive Directors are outlined below:
1. A reflective and thoughtful approach combined with an ability to offer considered advice based on sound judgement.
2. An individual of integrity, likely to be respected in their sector and peer group, demonstrating stature and gravitas.
3. An ability to probe incisively, to challenge effectively and constructively, and to offer support and guidance where appropriate.
4. An ability to build a successful working rapport with others around the board.
5. Well-developed communication skills, an ability to articulate complex ideas clearly, listen to others attentively and influence effectively.
6. An independence of mind, yet an ability to accept collective responsibility following full discussion and debate.
7. An ability to demonstrate an understanding and respect of the Executive / Non Executive boundaries.

In addition to these attributes, organisations will typically require specific skills and experience. These skills may be pertinent to the specific requirements of that Non Executive Director role and the committees that the Non Executive

Director is expected to contribute to (such as Audit, Remuneration, or Risk). The requirement may also include familiarity with the sector that the organisation operates in (such as financial services, life sciences or utilities) or revolve around the dynamics associated with product life cycle, business-to-business or business-to-consumer experience. Or it could be experience of operating in or developing business in specific geographies, developing digital product platforms, mergers and acquisitions experience, marketing and brand management expertise etc. Indeed the list of requirements can be endless.

In football (Soccer) a team doesn't play with five centre-forwards! Equally, ignorance of Board matters and areas of discussion at the Board table will hold you back. You will need to demonstrate a certain degree of financial awareness, be comfortable analysing the Profit and Loss and discussing balance sheet issues etc. For listed companies, you will also need to understand how the City and advisor community works and how companies use them, as well as understanding what and when you can say anything without infringing applicable legislation and regulation. Ignorance of finance is no defence.

The most effective Boards are those that bring together a diversity of experience, background and skills to complement the business as it competes now, and to position it as it faces the future. Non Executive Directors need to be able to rely on a broad base of experience rather than restrict their input to a relatively narrow area of expertise. Non Executive Directors need to have seen and done a lot. They need to have previously dealt with big issues and challenges and made the tough decisions.

Chapter 3: How to Become a Non Executive Director or Trustee

Non Executive Directors used to be caricatured as cronies of the Chairman (who is also a Non Executive Director) or CEO. Fat cats, freeloading members of the "old boy network", retirees who wanted to have somewhere to go other than the golf club for a decent lunch and a chat. Not an attractive scenario and for various reasons, but not least because of numerous serious corporate scandals where shareholders were left unprotected, the whole can of Non Executive worms has been subject to investigation, reappraisal and some rigorous new rulings.

Unlike Executive Directors who work for the organisation on a day to day basis, usually being responsible for particular functions such as finance, technology, marketing and so on, Non Executives have no line management responsibility but are there to ensure that the company is governed properly; that it complies with the right laws (of which there are many!), that its strategies are robust, that stakeholder interests are protected and subjected to the appropriate due diligence, particularly in the case of e.g. mergers or takeovers.

They are usually retained for a particular number of days per annum (which makes the knowledge part a little tricky when linked to accountability), they can serve for a particular period of time such as six years (i.e. two terms) and are sometimes paid but contrary to popular opinion are very often not paid anything other than their reasonable expenses.

A well chosen Non Executive Director can be key to good governance but getting that first NED appointment can be tricky.

I would advise people to look for a NED role while still serving as an executive. When you come out of your career, you can point to that NED position when seeking other roles.

How did I get my foot through the first door?

I visited head-hunters, networked all my contacts and spoke to every private equity firm I could get hold of.

A popular route to becoming a NED is to gain valuable experience serving as a school governor first. While the role is voluntary, governors have the same authority as a NED in a company.

Even a primary school may have a budget of £2m and 60 or 70 staff so all these issues related to running a business are within the school setting too.

The duties of the school governing board include appointing the head teacher, setting and controlling the budget, managing strategic direction and making sure the school delivers high-quality education. There is a huge need for school governors in the UK. There are 300,000 posts for governors in England and at any one time 40,000 of those positions are vacant.

Not every NED position will be advertised for open interview; the NED is the last bastion of the tap on the shoulder, but where they are, many interviewers don't understand the role of the NED.

The interviewer doesn't always know what they are looking for, so think about what you can bring to the board and improve the organisation. Quiz the chairman beforehand, what issues concern them and what are the big risk issues? Understand what you can do to improve the governance or the direction of the organisation.

What do Non Executive Directors do?

The size of the business and the nature of its business will have an impact of course on a Non-Exec's role. They may, however, have been recruited for a particular purpose or experience. For example, if a company is about to undertake a major change initiative, enter into a merger, trade in a new market or country or some other key transaction then they may be assigned particular duties around that, dealing with investor relations perhaps, mentoring the Executive Board on whether to accept an offer for their business and so on.

They may also sit on specialist committees related to remuneration, audit or talent management.

What seems to matter more is the way that Non-Execs carry out their duties if they are to succeed, add value and find the experience personally rewarding.

They must be independent minded, have integrity and the respect of the other board members, be prepared and able to look at the business from a "big picture" perspective, be well informed and manage difficult decisions in a facilitative manner.

The chemistry with others is vital. That doesn't mean being anyone's patsy or a push-over, it does mean conducting yourself in a mature and professional manner and being prepared to make a stand if you don't agree with the way things are being handled.

Why would you want to become a Non Executive Director or Trustee?

People become Non Executive Directors for various reasons. The pay is very often pretty low when you consider the risks and responsibility and the amount of work required of them. The work can expose them to risks of claims of negligence quite disproportionate to the rewards as we have seen in the recent banking crisis. Sometimes when they do ask the difficult questions, they might be moved out in a "board re-shuffle". Companies have to take out insurance to indemnify their Non Executive Directors against possible claims from the shareholders. You should never become a Non Executive Director without this insurance being in place.

At this point you might be wondering what the incentive is and how scary it all seems. Why would anyone want to sit on the board of an organisation as a Non Executive Director? What do they get out of it?

Happily, the concept of service is not entirely dead and buried. Some people want to give back to society something in return for the benefits they have reaped from their work. So, they may apply to serve on the board of their local Hospital, School or College. It can appeal to a person's sense of altruism too if they are serving on the boards of charities or not for profit organisations.

To a real businessperson, business is always fascinating and a Non Executive Directorship can keep one's hand in after the days of full executive responsibility have passed. Some see it as an opportunity to create a portfolio career of perhaps a couple of non-exec posts or maybe take on a Chairmanship. Not all roles as we have previously mentioned, however, carry remuneration and the demands are tough so this is by no means a soft option for the pre-retired.

If you have an ambitious eye to the future, it can also broaden your current executive experience in a particular sector which may prove beneficial to sharpening your leadership skills and career worth in a variety of ways. Some apparently just love the perceived kudos and other power and ego based experiences it brings them. It takes all sorts!

I suppose your next question is; provided I have the skills, how would I become one?

The routes tend to be rather different depending on whether it is a public sector appointment or whether it is for a private company or a listed company, either a mega FTSE corporation or smaller plc.

Public Sector

In the UK the post of Commissioner for Public Appointments was created in 1995 and is independent of both the Government and the Civil Service. In 2004/05 it oversaw the appointment of over 3,000 Non Executive posts; 38% of appointments made were women, 9% came from ethnic minorities and 4% were disabled. OPCA's Code of Practice states that all senior public appointments should be governed by the overriding principle of selection on merit.

They should be open to independent scrutiny and the recruitment process must be transparent and appointments are publicised openly. Search is often used proactively to ensure a strong list of interested candidates.

Private Sector

In the private sector our sources indicate that the situation is rather different. It really is a case of who you know and your perceived reputation and networks are of primary importance. High profile boards may apparently be reluctant to hire a "diverse" or "brave" candidate for fear of what City or media commentators will make of it, which just leads to more of the same within a closed circle of the elite. Privately owned firms tend not to get too hung up on that of course but they still tend to operate in a way that lacks real transparency and within favoured networks. Burnishing your reputation, canny networking and high profile speaking activities in the right circles can of course all help to create a trail to your door. Have a chat with your headhunting contacts to sound them out too.

Female Non Executive Director

According to a Deloitte report, among the top 350 firms, women make up only 3% of executive directors and 8% of Non Executives. The Female FTSE Report 2004 states that "Overall companies with women directors scored significantly higher (on corporate governance indicators) than companies with all male boards. There is clear evidence that better managed companies are those with gender diversity in their boardrooms". So, why are there not more women? Well why does the sun shine? There are plenty of lobbyists and compelling business cases out there for women to take on more senior roles in business and qualify for board appointments as either Exec or Non-Exec Directors but the old boy network and negative gender stereotypes linked to whether one has ovaries or not still prevail unfortunately. The tide will turn eventually and don't stop clamouring for the barriers to be broken down but be prepared for a tough ride. Try the Public Sector is our advice.

Chapter 4: Key Attributes Organisations Look for in Non Executive Director

A Non Executive Director needs good radar to fly at 30,000ft; to know when to go down to 3,000ft and when to come back up again.

"Choose your company with care and don't stray far from your domain of knowledge or comfort zone." – Ade Asefeso

A Non Executive Director should be on the Board of an organisation to add value, to challenge the Executive Directors on the strategy and direction of the business and ensure that the investment of the shareholders and broader stakeholders is being managed responsibly.

Before taking on a Non Executive role, it may be useful to understand what specific skills and experience you have and how you are perceived by others. You need to be clear what your criteria are for joining a company and how it plays to your strengths and interests. Be very clear about what you will learn and take away from the company and, as importantly, what is the added-value that you will give.

Similarly: Be clear what your point of difference is. If all the Non Executives bring similar background and experience, your ability to influence is much harder. In the same vein, a degree of familiarity with the sector that the company operates in and an affinity and empathy for the product is regarded by many as essential, especially for those taking on their first Non Executive Director role. Enthusiasm for the company, an interest and degree of knowledge of the sector is important, as individuals will be better able to translate their experience and perspectives. It is important to balance your interest in taking on a Non Executive role with ensuring that the role is the right one for you.

Don't get flattered. A friend of mine ended up accepting a role as a Non Executive Director and joined a board of a company operating in an industry that she knew nothing about and subsequently didn't enjoy the role. However, the more familiar you are with the sector, the greater the potential for conflict of interest and, where significant, such conflicts will present an insurmountable barrier to appointment. Obvious conflicts of interest include companies working in the same sector or providing a similar service, but equally conflicts can arise when company strategies collide and a strategic acquisition by one of your companies can create a conflict with another. Choose the company with extreme care and don't depart from your domain of knowledge or comfort zone.

The Importance of Due Diligence

Probably the most important task you need to complete prior to joining any Board is to undertake extensive due diligence. You need to ensure that you gain a comprehensive understanding of the business and the culture that pervades, its financial performance and funding, it strategy, and the experience, standing and reputation of the Executives and Chairman. Due diligence can take many forms, including speaking to the auditors, brokers and other advisors to the company.

I did withdraw from one opportunity the day before the appointment because I could not match the profit record with the management accounts cash flow. My timing was terrible and I felt I had let the Chairman down but the company was in administration within six months; so right decision, if awkward at the time. I have always started with cash flow since.

Some individuals enjoy the hands-on nature that a company in turnaround can present, and indeed their experience in corporate transformation or refinancing can be of huge benefit to a company facing significant issues; however, knowing that you are joining a company in turnaround is very different to discovering that you have unwittingly joined a sinking ship and the breakdown in trust and openness that is implied.

Use your own contacts and networks to sound out the opportunity with select individuals that you know and trust to gain their perspective on the company and its reputation. Speak informally to your contacts within their customer base or their suppliers to gain a wider picture and even to their competitors to develop a comprehensive picture on the company. I always speak try to speak to the previous Non Executive Directors if possible. History has a habit of repeating itself.

Chapter 5: Top Issues to Understand Before Accepting Appointments

As well as understanding the financial position of the company, the quality and balance of the Board is vital. Take time to understand the individuals concerned, their reputation, track record and the culture that prevails. Is it an open and transparent culture? Is the CEO open to being influenced? Is there an effective and constructive relationship between the CEO and Chairman? Do you understand their principles, priorities, ambitions and ego? Essentially, do you trust the key individuals concerned and is it a team you want to play for?

Due diligence checklist

Whilst not comprehensive, due diligence can include gaining information on the company, its financial position, strategy, principle risks and shareholder profile. As importantly, you need to do your own research on the key individuals concerned, their reputation, the quality of the Board and the culture that prevails. Due diligence is gained from a variety of sources including:

- Annual Reports
- Company Announcements
- Company website
- Analyst and Rating Agency Reports
- Company advisors including auditors, brokers, lawyers
- Press coverage
- Contacts you may have with the organisations competitors, suppliers or customers

- Previous directors of the company
- Shareholders

The induction programme

As a new Non Executive Director, you should take time to understand from the Chairman and the Company Secretary what the induction programme contains to enable you to get up to speed quickly with the key issues facing the company. An effective induction programme will take up considerable time during your first year as you visit the operational sites, meet and spend time with the Executive Directors and key management to understand the company better. Working with the Chairman to tailor your induction programme for your needs can be helpful. If functional specialists are crucial to the success of a company, make sure you make time to meet them to understand their key issues. For instance, if the company has a complicated debt structure, meet the Treasurer, Head of Tax etc.

Is the Board size effective? Too large and I will be one voice amongst many, too small and the demands on me will be greater.

You will need to have read the previous Board minutes, understand the key projects and priorities that the Board are considering and the nature and personalities of your fellow Board colleagues. If you are new to the listed environment, you may need additional support to understand the dynamics and interactions of the various advisors in and around the Board. If you are less experienced in financial management, spend more time with the CFO (Chief Finance Officer) to understand the key issues to enable you to contribute rather than feel as if you are staring into a void. Many of the larger audit firms run training programmes and seminars on a range of issues pertinent to Non Executive Directors.

You also need to ensure that you understand the board committees, risk management policies and procedures and that you are covered by the company's Directors and Officers (D&O) liability insurance. The Company Secretary will often be at hand to provide you with all the information you require and the Chairman is often actively involved in ensuring that you, as a new Non Executive Director, are able to understand the business and their issues quickly to enable you to contribute effectively.

What to do... Think carefully when choosing your first Non Executive Director position; it plays a crucial role in shaping your future portfolio. Realising your ambition to be a Non Executive Director is often a great achievement in itself. However, ensuring that you are successful in transitioning effectively to the role is often easier said than done. Based on the wide-ranging experience and advice provided by the experienced Non Executive Directors and Chairman who have contributed to this Book, we highlight some of the attributes that successful Non Executive Directors tend to demonstrate:

1. A degree of self-knowledge; they know who they are and how they are perceived by others.
2. Team spirit, with a low ego and a desire to make others successful, rather than themselves.
3. Strong and effective relationship management skills. Being a Non Executive Director is a unique role. You come together a few times a year with people from different backgrounds, agendas and styles and need to be able to fit in quickly and contribute effectively.
4. Ease and comfort in handling ambiguity.

5. Self-confident style yet ability to demonstrate humility.
6. Willingness to take the tough decisions.
7. Lack of embarrassment about asking the simple questions.
8. An enthusiasm for and an interest in the business.
9. Patience and an ability to "seed and water" an idea. It's all about emotional intelligence; the ability to listen, challenge constructively and build trust with your fellow directors quickly.
10. An interest in strategy, people and performance.
11. Intelligence, incisiveness and an ability to identify the key issues and priorities quickly.
12. Financial literacy and good analytical skills based on data and fact combined with an experienced "sense of smell".
13. Independence of the Executive Directors and of the Chairman and there on their own merits.
14. Ability to effectively balance the challenge and supportive nature of the role.
15. Ability to think strategically.
    - Brains – strong analytical skills and the ability to understand complex issues...
    - Bravery – strong in questioning and perseverance if not happy with the response...
    - Balance – be pragmatic, the world is not a perfect place.

    ...and what not to do...

However, like it or not, some individuals are less suited to the role of a Non Executive Director. The habits and behaviours they tend to demonstrate that are less well received include:
1. Not being prepared for the Board meeting, neither having read the papers nor understood the issues.

2. Lack of contribution to the debate; does the Non Executive Director not understand the issue, are they not engaged or just not interested in the company?
3. A tendency to talk too much, hog the debate, pontificate or show little care for others' opinion. The worse type of Non Executive Director is a failed executive who is trying to score points off the Executives.
4. If they are too hesitant, nervous or cautious.
5. If they stray into the Executives territory, telling rather than influencing.
6. Not appreciating the difference between opinion and fact.
7. Sulking when they lose an argument. It's a job and those who do not approach it as such are the ones to watch out for.
8. Frequently distracted by Blackberries or emails.
9. Becoming identified with a singular agenda and cannot let it go.
10. Not commanding the respect of their peers. A raised eyebrow or a distinct change of tone when a Non Executive speaks is a warning sign that they have lost the respect of the Board.

Chapter 6: Becoming Non Executive Director

How becoming a Non Executive Director could help your career

Many professionals with portfolio careers become Non Executive Directors to gain extra experience and income. We will discuss how to secure the position and balance the workload in this chapter.

Over the last decade there has been a growth in portfolio careers a living derived from have multiple simultaneous jobs on a part-time, flexible, consulting or interim basis.

Those juggling such careers cite the positives that derive from having exciting variety or the better work-life balance and greater flexibility afforded by being their own boss. What is not often mentioned is the constant strain of keeping all these plates spinning while securing the next piece of work; a magic trick some seem to achieve effortlessly while others toil and sweat.

Often a useful way some portfolioists derive a more reliable income stream is by including one or two remunerated Non Executive Director (NED) positions. Such roles not only benefit them by providing a regular salary, but also help develop skills, profile and credibility in other lines of work.

NEDs sit on the board of many public, private and not-for-profit organisations, working as a critical friend scrutinising the organisation's performance and offering strategic input and advice to the executive team. How often they meet and what duties they are required to perform varies between organisations.

NEDs can, however, expect at least a monthly commitment to attend meetings (having read the necessary board reports), plus further meetings if appointed to a sub-committee dealing with specific issues such as remuneration and finance. They may be required to be present at public events, such as an opening of a new building, and some boards also provide training and team development away-days that will require a time commitment (sometimes overnight).

A friend of mine, for instance, runs a consultancy company; she is chair of drugs and alcohol abuse treatment service provider, deputy chair of governors for a university and NED of an NHS primary care trust. She aims for a mix of three days a week of interim project commitments with two days as an NED a mix she admits is sometimes hard to achieve and maintain.

The opportunity to connect with an organisation on a long-term basis as it develops and goes on a journey has made her appreciate the dynamics and tensions that can exist between boards and executive teams. This has benefited her interim project work because clients see her as someone who understands the strategic not just operational needs and can speak to all the key stakeholders.

Breaking through into the Non Executive world and achieving the first post can be tricky. Often people wanting to be NEDs face the experience/opportunity catch-22 that many first-time job seekers and graduates encounter can't get a job because without the experience but can't get the experience without the job. Boards appointing new NEDs are often looking to find people that already have experience of how a board operates and know how a good NED can make a difference.

A good way to start is to seek out quasi-board positions, such as sitting on strategic partnership teams above projects being delivered by organisations in joint-venture partnerships. This will give you experience of what it's like to offer strategic input and vision while not having direct executive responsibility for the project.

You could also secure a non-remunerated NED role. These posts are usually found in public, not-for-profit or third sector organisations such as social landlords, charities and community groups. They are a great way to get a foothold in the Non Executive market and prove you have the skills to be an active board member.

Many NEDs find that once they have that first board-level role under their belt, they can access further Non Executive opportunities more easily. They are more firmly on the radar of organisations seeking new board members as well as other interim or portfolio work.

Our advice for those seeking a first step into the world of NEDs is; "in the first instance, be persistent and keep at it and once you are up and running, keep your different things separate. I use a number of web tools to keep my papers in the cloud and manage my time."

It should also be noted that boards will sometimes seek out new members with certain skills and backgrounds that may be required by the organisation at that point in time. For instance, a Non Executive board member with a finance background may be of more interest if there is an audit or executive salary review due. The NEDs won't be expected to roll their sleeves up and help deliver operational challenges but they will be expected to ask the right questions of the executive team to safeguard the health and performance of the organisation on behalf of its staff, stakeholders and customers.

Taking on an NED role while also maintaining a portfolio career can be a tricky balancing act. Boards will have established and non-negotiable meeting dates, which you will be expected to commit to, and this can create tension when clients come calling with new or extra work. Many NEDs talk of the need to find a balance of commitment. They are regularly tested by the dilemma of accepting another NED position that can provide a steady income, intellectual interest and a bit of kudos while also holding out for that next big (and possibly more lucrative) chunk of interim or project work that will require blood, sweat, tears. But if that balance can be achieved the benefits to a career portfolioist can be very rewarding.

Chapter 7: Using Non Executive Directors to Expand Your Executive Universe

Indian Perspective

Every Indian enterprise today faces a talent shortage of one kind or another. The challenge faced by mid-sized businesses with revenues in the range of US$250 million to US$500 million is particularly acute. Having successfully survived the start-up phase and developed the critical mass of a going concern, they are now focused on moving up to the next level. This brings the Chief Executive Officer (CEO) often the promoter who founded the firm a new set of goals; expanding into new markets, becoming a dominant player in the industry and increasing revenue ten or twenty-fold.

Achieving these objectives, of course, usually requires a senior management team different than the one the firm has in place. While the current team, which is likely to have been with the company since its earliest stages, may well have the operational skill to manage an SME, they are unlikely to have the strategic vision and experience to grow the company to the US$2 billion to $US5 billion level. So CEO then looks to identify a Chief Financial Officer, a Chief Information Officer or a Chief Operating Officer who has the necessary track record and gravitas to do so.

At this point, many CEOs meet with frustration and find that despite their best efforts they are unable to successfully recruit the executives they need. Indeed, they often find that it is more difficult to attract qualified candidates when the company revenue is US$500 million than when it was US$50 million. The reason is that at this point the company is no longer competing for talent against other SMEs but rather against well-known, elite consulting and financial services firms and multinational companies, whether based in India or abroad. Even if the smaller firm can compete in terms of salary and growth potential, its company brand lacks the recognition and status of its larger rivals. (This particularly is the case when the smaller firm is in the B2B sector and located outside the major metropolitan cities or commercial hubs, working behind the scenes to supply its high-profile B2C customers.) And because lower brand recognition of the employer is perceived to translate into lower social and professional recognition of the employee, top-tier candidates often do not view the smaller firm as an attractive career option.

Solving most problems caused by scarcity requires savvier use of the available resources, and this case is no exception. Despite the attention paid in the past few years to the issue of corporate governance, most Indian firms regard the board of directors as a regulatory obligation rather than a strategic resource. But for SMEs looking to recruit the management talent they need to reach the next level, the board can be a powerful tool.

Most Indian CEOs choose their Non Executive Directors (NEDs) from within their close circle of friends, acquaintances and business relationships. It is understandable that CEO would want to be surrounded with executives whom he or she knows, trusts and shares social ties. But choosing NEDs in this way adds only marginal value to the experience base and professional network from which the company can draw. Indeed, a NED seat is the perfect opportunity to involve exactly the top-tier talent that an SME needs, in the form of retired or soon-to-be-retired CEOs of firms at the level to which the company aspires. While the demand for top-tier senior executives far exceeds the supply, the traditional Indian concept of retirement provides relatively little opportunity for retired CEOs to pass along their experience in a structured and meaningful way. This amounts to a squandering of resources, given the vast knowledge and wisdom these CEOs accumulated as they successfully paved the way in the liberalized and competitive new India. These corporate leaders are now in a position to share their valuable experience with those who are willing to ask.

In addition to a new source of seasoned strategic counsel, the SME CEO gains two additional benefits from viewing the board in this way. First, taking a more deliberate approach to board composition sends a message to the business community and potential candidates that the company is committed to becoming a global player follows best practices and is capable of attracting top-tier talent. More importantly, however, a board that includes strategically chosen NEDs significantly expands the professional network from which CEO can recruit and increases the firm's strength. These NEDs act as "forces of attraction" that pull both public awareness and top-level talent to the business.

A recently retired CEO of a large concern, after all, will have numerous highly-placed protégés throughout the industry over which he or she retains considerable influence. Once these new directors have settled into their roles, it would not be unreasonable to ask them to find one or two candidates they think would be appropriate for a particular management position. Of course, it will be important to screen those candidates against external, objective benchmarks and industry standards to guide the final selection and ensure the best fit. Well-chosen NEDs can give a company privileged access to candidates it would not normally have and serve as a powerful endorsement of the company to those candidates in today's highly competitive environment.

Chapter 8: The Role of Non Executive Board Directors Today

There has been, at least in the past, a misconception in the business community that Non Executive Directors are somehow subject to less stringent duties of care to the companies that they are involved with. That is simply not the case. Any non-exec still labouring under that false belief could be heading for trouble.

Of course, breach of director's duties (executive and non-execs alike) has far reaching consequences; such as the threat of director disqualification proceedings and personal liability for misfeasance.

Whilst non-execs cannot be expected to have the same detailed knowledge and experience of a company's affairs as executive directors due to the time invested in fulfilling the role, in determining whether a non-exec has breached his or her duty to exercise reasonable care, skill and diligence, a court will consider the steps which ought to have been taken by a reasonably diligent non-exec to familiarise themselves with the company's business and operations.

Below are recommendations for best practice both prior to joining a board and on appointment to a board. It is essential reading for all existing and potential non-execs.
1. Exercise judgment to become satisfied on the culture, values and behaviours associated with the board.
2. Understand that your role is to provide independence, oversight and constructive challenge to the board.

3. Ensure you receive a schedule of future board and committee meetings planned well in advance so that you have the opportunity to attend.
4. Insist on receiving high-quality information regarding the company's affairs which is clear, comprehensive and up-to-date sufficiently in advance of meetings.
5. Speak to the executive directors, or if necessary, the company's professional advisers, over any concerns but take independent professional advice at the company's expense if you consider that necessary to discharge your responsibilities.
6. Ensure you make all decisions objectively in the interests of the company and that your independent judgment is not affected upon any reliance on income received from the appointment.
7. Understand that circumstances may arise which require you to consider resigning from the board and take independent advice where necessary.

As a Non Executive board director, I have been thinking a lot lately about what it means to do this role in today's environment. With a dramatically different economic climate in which organisations are now operating, as well as increased scrutiny by stakeholders and governments alike, the nature of what it takes to be a responsible board member, too, has changed. Simply looking over the shoulder of the executive team and offering an occasional word of wisdom or direction is not sufficient. Non Executive board directors today need to be activist in their approach to ensuring that the organisations they serve do not simply survive but thrive, even in economically difficult conditions. The boards on which they serve should demand no less of them than that.

The best organisations of all sizes, in the for-profit and not-for profit sectors alike, are looking for active, engaged, independent, and interested board members and they encourage a climate in which having those people on the board can bear fruit. These board rooms are environments in which board members are comfortable, and indeed required, to ask hard questions, challenge the status quo, and step up to assist in areas where they can. An independent board of director should bring independence in word and deed and a fresh perspective to the organisation.

How does this manifest itself in practice?

Understanding relationships and roles of the stakeholders is vital. Non Executive Directors need to be able to distinguish between different types of relationship within and outside the organisation, as well as see the connections between them; relationships between the board and the senior executive team, the organisation's staff, and investors relationships with the organisation's customers and the market in which it operates, including partners and competitors; and fellow board members.

How does this translate into an activist approach?

Activist board directors engage and reach out. They ask questions inside and outside the organisation and seek advice from fellow board members, senior executives, staff and investors and thus gain a fuller understanding of the challenges their organisation confronts, as well as the resources and capabilities it has (and needs) to master them. In my experience, this implies a number of different strategies.

First, and especially at the point when joining as a new director, I have found it incredibly useful to reach out to existing directors and get to know them beyond their bios and outside of the structured board setting. Getting to know my fellow Executive and Non Executive board of directors and understanding what their passion for the organisation is and where it comes from, how and why they have made the organisation part of themselves, helps to build board cohesion and can make a big difference in avoiding confusion in the heat of the board room. Boards function better when the people around the table know and trust one another and feel that they are moving in the same direction.

Second, this focus on people does not stop at the board level. It is essential that today's board directors engage much more broadly. Being approachable and reaching out to people, they are able to talk with, and especially to listen to, senior managers, staff, and investors, understand and respect their views, and help harnessing their passion and commitment to the organisation, thus ensuring its endurance and robustness. Hearing the voices from the organisation directly means Non Executives board members can form their own ideas and perspectives on the information they are receiving in board papers and reports.

Third, people focus, as important as it is, is not all that distinguishes activist directors. Understanding the nuts and bolts of the business also means, and indeed requires, asking the hard questions. It also means not being satisfied with simply asking the questions, but doing something with the answers. An independent perspective here means being sensitive to internal factors that shape the organisation's capacity to survive and thrive as it confronts current challenges and those that will surely arise in the future. I have a special interest in finance and the audit committee, so for me that means being comfortable asking hard questions about the numbers, past, present, and future.

Fourth, though the nuts and bolts of the organisation are internal, they do not exist in isolation from the outside world. Non Executive board of directors need to keep an eye on the global factors that shape the broader environment in which their organisation operates; from government regulation to customer expectations and to a constantly changing competitive landscape. This outside independent perspective is indeed one of the greatest values board members can bring to the table. Keeping on top of these developments is not always easy, but it is necessary, and, in our electronically and humanly networked world, possible. Again, one element is to proactively seek knowledge, the other, and equally important one, is to do something with it; to seek and see opportunities for the organisation to shape the environment in which it operates.

To bring things back to the board room, sensitivity to local and global issues, internal and external matters, and understanding the human and material assets of the organisation are core aspects of the activist approach. Yet, they can only be useful if Non Executive board of directors are also part of creating a safe environment for open, critical, constructive conversation to move the organisation to the next level.

Because today's healthy board rooms are becoming places of active and rigorous discussion, Non Executive Directors must also contribute to sustaining a constructive environment by avoiding abusing the space it creates. I have been lucky to be in board rooms with some directors who have mastered the art of communicating effectively in the board room setting; not holding back opinions if something is obviously wrong, but also waiting for the right time to say things. And not just say things in ways that are comfortable for themselves, but say them in ways they will be heard and listened to. Above all, they do not just say things for their own sake, but because they are important and add value to a discussion that is focused on benefitting the organisation and not the individual that says something.

In a nut shell, as an active, engaged, and accountable non executive board member in today's board room, I constantly strive to have the best possible understanding of the business the organisation is in and the one it wants to be in, and what the organisation is and what it wants to be. On that basis I can help devise feasible and viable strategies to get from one to the other and contribute to guiding the organisations on whose boards I sit into a successful and sustainable future and do the job I have been hired to do.

Chapter 9: Public and Not for Profit Non Executive Director

Non Executive Directors on the boards of public sector organisations bring their broad experience, as well as specific knowledge and functional expertise. Non-Executives work as members of the board team with the executive members (such as the Chief Executive, Finance Director and HR Director).

The key responsibilities of a Non Executive Director are:
1. Contributing to the delivery of strong organisational governance, ensuring the organisation is operating in the public interest and in a transparent and ethical way to fulfil its objectives.
2. Helping to plan for the future to improve services and organisational effectiveness.
3. Ensuring that the management team meets its key performance targets and holding it to account.
4. Ensuring that the finances of the organisation are managed properly with accurate, robust information.
5. Helping the Board to keep its stakeholders and customers properly informed.
6. Serving on important board committees.

Non Executive Directors are usually expected to commit between 1 to 4 days per month depending on the sector and type of organisation. This time can comprise a range of different activities from Board meetings, committee meetings, discussions with the Chief Executive and/or other directors, ambassadorial duties (e.g. fundraising events) and meetings with regulatory or performance bodies. However it can also comprise the time involved in preparing for meetings and undertaking essential background reading.

The remuneration level for Non Executive Directors varies depending on sector, scale of organisation and time commitment.

Charities and Government Departments are under pressure to deliver more services but struggling due to funding reductions, research has shown.

According to the latest survey report from A Global Sourcing Ltd are findings shows that charities and government departments are in a "perfect storm".

The research showed that 69% of charities and government departments are under pressure to deliver more services, but are clearly struggling in light of funding reductions. Many are facing an acute funding crisis. The report highlights that charities and government departments have experienced a net reduction in income across all funding streams, with 63% having been negatively affected by the government's spending cuts. It also says that 20% are considering a potential merger, and 28% are looking at reducing headcount, even though the sector saw rise in job losses last year.

Another coping strategy for some organisations is to step up fundraising efforts; 66% plan to increase fundraising activity, even though the majority of charities (93%) said the fundraising climate is tougher than ever, and 65% plan to expand into new areas.

According to Cass Business School, charities lost £23m in assets during the downturn. The UK's biggest 500 fundraising charities saw their collective investment fund value drop by 21.4 per cent, while there was an 8.4 per cent decline in income received from charity investments.

On a more positive note, we saw the launch of the £600m Big Society Capital fund to boost the social investment market and the announcement of details of its first investment commitments of £37m to 12 organisations out of the 130 that had originally applied.

However, with 171,000 registered charities in the UK, the funds are helping very few organisations in reality. Another problem is that many charities don't have the right people with the right skills to help them access these new funding streams and prepare them for this kind of investment.

Another option for charities with trading arms is to hire non-executive directors and/or trustees with specialist commercial experience who could help them trade out of this financial crisis while meeting their charitable objectives. Such individuals could also help to put their organisation in a better position to access these new funding opportunities.

About half of charity and most of social enterprise income comes through trading, whether that is through running shops or through government contracts. Unsurprisingly, many charities understand that building this income could be the route out of this crisis. However, many are starting to recognise the need to hire commercial experts onto their boards.

Over the past year, head-hunters have seen a demand on services to help recruit NEDs for various organisations, including charity trading subsidiaries and social enterprises and NHS. While they may sit alongside the trustees from the main board of the organisation, they will focus purely on the commercial interests of the organisation. They will ensure the organisation is trading properly, that its financial interests are being well served, that it is being run in accordance with the law, and, most importantly, that it is generating profit. I'm sure that soon we will start to see a greater numbers of NEDs being recruited specifically to help charities and social enterprises understand whether or not they can benefit from Big Society Capital.

Another key aspect of the Ned role is as a contract negotiator. In our experience, NEDs are less likely to have an emotional attachment to the organisation than typical trustees and are, therefore, likely to be more effective negotiators who can secure good contract terms; however, just as organisations struggle to find trustees from diverse backgrounds, it can prove even harder to find suitable NEDs with the right commercial experience because such people tend not to be known within existing networks.

Chapter 10: Start-ups Non Executive Director

What seems to be notable amongst the huge number of start up businesses is that there is an underlying and somewhat unspoken feeling that it doesn't matter how many businesses start-up, it is how many succeed and this is a sentiment shared by almost everyone I have spoken to over the past few months.

Non-Executive Directors may well prove key to help change this unspoken feeling. What a young and inexperienced management team or entrepreneur does not have is the benefit of hindsight and this is key to growing a successful business, ensuring that the growth is controlled, the direction is planned and more importantly the same old pitfalls are avoided.

How to find the right non-executive director for your business

The increased scrutiny that boards are facing, both public and private, means that simply tapping into the 'old boy's network' will not necessarily deliver the best candidate. Recruiting an independent director needs to be carefully thought through. Don't limit your sights. The best person may not be an experienced NED, but have the technical or functional skills to take your board to the next level.

Define your needs

The motivation for having a NED on your board needs to be clear. If you are just looking for someone to help with business development, then a NED is not necessarily that person. Questions you should ask include; what experience is mandatory, and what balance of experience is required vis-à-vis other directors?

Identify specific characteristics

Add value to your board by making sure you are clear about expectations. What technical or functional areas do you need to address? How much time is realistically required? What do you want to know from referees? How will you assess suitability?

Know your company

Can you objectively describe your company and challenges? Any prospective NED will want to do a thorough job of due diligence on the role and company. Ensure you can accurately describe your strengths and weaknesses, likely strategic challenges and financial health. It will not be unusual for candidates to want to meet your outside advisors or key investors.

Search thoroughly

It is highly likely that your board or business colleagues will be able to suggest possible candidates from existing networks. However, try to avoid rushing for the easiest option. Instead, look for cost-effective alternatives. It is a critical role and throwing the net as wide as possible will pay dividends.

Internet searching can be a good place to start as there are a number of databases available. However, if you are uncertain about your requirements, or how to go about shortlisting potential candidates, a recruitment consultant should be able to help. Some sites will recommend reliable recruiters.

Be robust from start to finish

From selection to appointment, it can be tempting to rush at the end once you've found your ideal NED. All candidates should be assessed according to your objective criteria. You might consider interviewing in both an informal and formal setting changing the venue can reveal a lot about a candidate's personality.

Accelerate their learning

Once on board, a planned induction process will help you and your new NED. Visits to facilities and meetings with staff and customers will benefit you both, quickly helping the NED to settle in and be effective.

Chapter 11: Start-ups Guide to Managing Non Executive Directors

Can problems arise?

It is very important to draw firm ground rules as a strong-minded non executive could take over if allowed particularly if they are very experienced and you are just starting out. And it probably won't be intentional which makes controlling it all the more important.

Choose someone you think will fit in well as you would someone to work in a small team in the office. You won't be seeing them everyday but they will be taking part in important decisions that affects everyone day to day, which amounts to the same thing.

Make it clear in the contract the number of days they will be expected to attend but also stipulate a maximum number of days. It is unlikely someone with other interests will want to spend all their time with you; but you want to guard against a fatal attraction situation where they can't stay away. Remember that this is a contract like any other. If you clearly lay down your expectations and they lay down theirs there is no reason why anything should go wrong. And most importantly, with a pre determined period of notice, either one of you can walk away. If you don't like them, terminate the contract; odds on they will be quick to do the same.

When should you employ a non-exec?

There is no set time when you should employ a non exec. But equally it is all too easy to go along and assume you are managing very well without one. It is a good idea to have your board and systems in place if only so they have some board meetings to attend.

You might take someone on when you are looking at a change in direction. This might be in terms of expansion or if you are trying to appeal to a different market. In this case you will have a clear idea of the objectives but could have run out of the knowledge and the contacts to achieve them.

A common barrier to this can be the expense, though. But as we know, this is only a part time position and need not actually cost you that much. And when you combine the salary with a stake in the business, you may not actually have to expend that much anyway.

And while it can happen, you would be unlucky in your choice of non exec if the value they added to company in terms of experience wasn't worth the cost. Gift horses and mouths come into mind!

Chapter 12: Executive and Non Executive Directors Responsibilities by Law

Directors of companies whether public or private have various responsibilities towards their companies, breach of which may not only be detrimental to those companies and their shareholders but also may lead to civil and criminal liability of the individual director concerned.

Executive and Non Executive Directors have the same responsibilities in law. An Executive Director is a director who has separate responsibilities within the company as an Executive. The role of a Non Executive Director has a positive contribution to making and ensuring that the board fulfils its main objectives. He can exercise an impartial influence and bring to bear experience gained from other fields; executive directors would therefore be well advised to consider the appointment of such directors to serve alongside them.

Powers of Directors

Directors derive their power from the Articles of Association and the Memorandum of Association. Directors must exercise their powers collectively and majority decisions will prevail.

Duties of Directors

The duties of directors are owed to the company as a whole. Their duties and responsibilities arise both out of common law and out of statute and can be classified as follows:-
1. Fiduciary duty to act honestly and in good faith.
2. Duty to exercise skill and care.
3. Statutory duty.

Directors should bear in mind that breach of these duties may result in their being judged unfit to be concerned in the management of a company and lead to their disqualification as directors.

Fiduciary Duty

Four separate rules have emerged:-
1. Directors must act in good faith in what they believe to be the best interests of the company. Generally speaking, the interests of the company are to be equated with the interests of its members as a whole. As between different groups of shareholders, the directors must act fairly.
2. Directors must exercise their power only for the purpose for which they were granted.
3. Directors must not place themselves in a position in which there is a conflict between their duties to the company and the personal interest or duties to others.
4. Directors must not fetter their discretion by agreeing, either with one another or with third parties, how to vote at future board meetings. However, that does not prevent them from committing the company to a contract which requires further action at subsequent board meetings.

Duty of Skill and Care

Responsibilities of directors include taking reasonable steps to ensure that the company's assets are properly collected, safeguarded, insured and invested, and that all payments are supported by proper documentation. Directors are required in the performance of their duties:-

1. To exhibit such a degree of skill as may reasonably be expected from a person with their knowledge and experience.
2. To take such care as an ordinary person might be expected to take on their own behalf. In applying these standards no distinction is to be drawn between executive and Non Executive Directors.
3. Executive directors should devote their time and energy to company matters in accordance with the terms of their contract. In most cases this will require them to devote all their working time.
4. Non Executive Directors are not required to give continuous attention to company affairs. However, they should familiarise themselves with the company's affairs including its financial position and should attend meetings of the board whenever they are reasonably able to do so.
5. Were a director, whether executive or non executive, has a particular skill for example he is a qualified accountant, he should exhibit the skill or ability reasonably expected from a person in that profession.

Statutory Duty

Company law imposes a number of duties on directors for example the preparation of the Annual Financial Statements.

Duty to Employees

As an employer the company must comply with the requirements of employment law. The directors, being in charge of the management of the company's affairs, should have this in mind when dealing with employment matters.

Duties in relation to Auditors

With the exception of companies exempt from audit, it is the duty of the company in general meeting to appoint auditors for each financial year. Auditors of a private company are deemed to be reappointed each year if an elective resolution not to reappoint auditors annually is in force.

Auditors have a statutory right of access at all times to the company's books, the accounts and vouchers and to require from the officers and from the company such information as is necessary for the performance of their duties. Directors must therefore ensure that the auditors have adequate information for the performance of their duties.

Equal standards of care

A board of directors acts as a whole and although some of its members may be given additional powers by the articles or by resolution, the general duties and responsibilities are the same for each director. There is no distinction between the position of executive and Non Executive Directors. If a breach of duty is to be attributed to a board on the basis that all of its members were present at a meeting which had approved a wrongful act, then the liability of each director is joint and several and no allowance is made for the fact that some are part timers and may have acquiesced in a situation which they did not fully understand.

For these purposes the directors are in the same position as trustees of a fund and may be held liable for knowledge of wrong doings in relation to dealings with its property. Higher duties are owed by those who are employed under service contracts or because of professional skill.

Remuneration of Non Executive Directors

Non Executive Directors should be adequately compensated for the time that they spent on the company's business. It is important that the Non Executive Directors should not be reliant on the company for a significant part of their income otherwise their independence may be jeopardised.

If a non executive has an executive appointment elsewhere, he may be required to pay the fees he receives to the employing company. There is an implication that if a person is engaged full time elsewhere he should not be permitted to sit part time on the board of a different organisation and not be separately remunerated. Whether the service contract with their principal employer allows him this flexibility is a question of fact rather than law. If the director is a partner in a professional firm there is usually an obligation to account for any earnings and benefits to the partnership.

Chapter 13: Boards Led by Non Executive Chairmen

This chapter is meant to help boards led by non executive chairmen understand the defining activities and attributes of the best CEO-board relationships; relationships that consistently contribute to organizational performance and superior results.

Our goal in this chapter is twofold: To provide boards and CEOs with a clear understanding of the essential elements of an effective CEO-board relationship and to enable boards and CEOs to both assess and improve their current performance in delivering against each of these relationship attributes. We have identified 25 essential elements of an effective CEO-board relationship, each with an actionable defining standard. We hope these prove useful in assessing the health and quality of the relationship dynamics in your organisation.

Relationship Responsibilities of the Non Executive Chairman

1. **Effectively advises CEO:** The chairman serves as a critical mentor and advisor to CEO. Beyond an ability to advice on the content of strategic decisions, the chairman provides thoughtful, actionable guidance on how to effectively translate strategy into action. The chairman maintains an open-door policy for CEO to seek guidance.

2. **Asks tough questions:** The chairman asks probing, penetrating questions on the logic of strategic decisions

and the dynamics of organizational performance. The chairman consistently demonstrates the courage to ask tough questions.

3. **Acts when necessary:** The chairman doesn't hesitate to act when the standards of governance and fiduciary responsibility require intervention. The chairman is willing to get his/her "hands dirty" when circumstances require a hands-on approach (e.g., crisis management).

4. **Maintains right attitude on strategy and succession:** The chairman owns and embraces an active leadership role in CEO succession. The chairman makes clear that he/she will play a critical role in leading the board discussion on approving strategy but that he/she won't attempt to take over CEO's responsibility for developing strategy.

5. **Demonstrates full commitment and engagement:** The chairman maintains and demonstrates a deep commitment to the performance of the organization, and this commitment clearly is reflected in his/her level of engagement on issues of critical importance to the performance of the firm. The chairman brings a spirit of energetic teamwork to all interactions with CEO.

6. **Collaborates with CEO to establish expectations, agendas, processes and decision rules:** The chairman is clear on the board's expectations of CEO. The chairman collaborates with CEO and seeks his/her input in establishing board agendas, processes and decision rules. The chairman sets precise expectations on the inputs upon which the board needs to make decisions.

7. **Proactively seeks to build professional relationships with management team:** The chairman seeks to build professional relationships with key members of the management team. The chairman has keen insight into the profiles (backgrounds, personalities, capabilities) of these critical executives.

8. **Effectively communicates and facilitates:** The chairman is always available and communicates openly, proactively and transparently with CEO and directors. The chairman is uniquely able to facilitate useful discussions with CEO and the board. The chairman encourages forceful discussions yet manages the dialog toward positive outcomes.

Relationship Responsibilities of CEO

9. **Informally builds relationships with board members:** CEO proactively works to communicate and build relationships with the chairman and directors via regular, informal interactions outside of board meetings. CEO uses these interactions not only to share information and gather input but also to develop strong "professional chemistry" with each member of the board.

10. **Communicates openly, proactively and transparently:** CEO maintains a strict "no surprises" policy with the board. CEO is fully and effortlessly transparent on the implications and risks of strategic decisions.

11. **Proactively seeks board input outside of board meetings:** Outside of board meetings, with the knowledge of the chairman, CEO actively and informally seeks board members' informal input, feedback and

guidance on strategy. When CEO presents strategies for approval, he or she is able to predict (and acknowledge) likely areas of disagreement with individual board members.

12. **Provides exposure to the executive team:** CEO facilitates informal introductions between members of the board and members of the management team. To facilitate succession planning, CEO frequently brings members of the management team to board meetings, where managers play a substantive role. CEO encourages board members to advise key managers on issues tied to their specific areas of expertise.

13. **Fully commits to the idea of an independent board:** CEO is fully committed to the concept of an independent chairman and board. CEO accepts the board's role in choosing his/her successor and actively supports succession management. CEO partners with the chairman to strengthen the board. CEO works to avoid the development of board factions.

14. **Balances strong points of view with open mindedness and flexibility:** CEO communicates clear, compelling points of view but also demonstrates uninhibited willingness to fully consider and apply the board's views. CEO encourages the board to challenge his/her assumptions. CEO effectively challenges the assumptions of board members.

15. **Recognizes the power of complementary skills on the board:** CEO recognizes the value of a board populated by individuals with skills and perspectives that are distinct from (and complementary to) his or her own.

CEO feels strengthened by board members who maintain skills/expertise that are superior to his or her own. CEO doesn't play politics with the board.

Relationship Responsibilities of Directors

16. **Effectively advises CEO:** Directors advise on the substance of strategic decisions. Directors provide thoughtful, actionable guidance on how to effectively translate strategy into action. Directors maintain an open-door policy for CEO to seek guidance.

17. **Asks tough questions:** Directors ask probing, penetrating questions on the logic of strategic decisions and the dynamics of organizational performance. Directors consistently demonstrate the courage to ask tough questions.

18. **Acts when necessary:** With the agreement of the chairman, directors don't hesitate to act when the standards of governance and fiduciary responsibility require intervention. Directors are willing to get their "hands dirty" when circumstances require a hands-on approach (e.g., crisis management).

19. **Demonstrates full commitment and engagement:** Directors maintain a deep commitment to the performance of the organization, and this commitment clearly is reflected in their level of engagement on issues of critical importance to the performance of the firm. Directors bring a spirit of energetic teamwork to all interactions with CEO.

Shared Relationship Responsibilities

20. **Commits to act in best interests of the firm:** All parties recognize and embrace their obligation to work in the best interests of the firm.

21. **Builds close but independent relationships:** All parties work to build robust professional relationships but ensure that these relationships demonstrate the independence required for CEO to do his or her job and for the board to maintain objectivity in reviewing CEO's recommendations and performance.

22. **Establishes precise expectations:** All parties set distinct expectations for themselves and for each other. All parties establish clear objectives. All parties keep their promises.

23. **Establishes distinct roles and responsibilities:** All parties maintain clearly defined and communicated roles and responsibilities. All parties are completely knowledgeable about their own responsibilities and the responsibilities of their counterparts.

24. **Demonstrates humility, self-awareness and a "low-ego approach":** All parties bring a genuine level of intellectual and professional humility to each interaction. All parties are self-aware of their strengths, weaknesses and limitations. All parties are comfortable with having their ideas rigorously challenged.

25. **Demonstrates honesty, trust, respect and transparency:** All parties work to establish relationships characterized by the highest standards of honesty,

trustworthiness, respect and transparency. All parties work to create an environment characterized by mutual respect. All parties are fully transparent regarding their opinions, plans and underlying motivations.

We wrote this chapter with the input of sitting CEOs, chairmen and directors from a range of industry sectors and regions to provide guidance and structure for boards as they assess the clarity of their roles and the effectiveness of their relationships across the board as a whole. The 25 essential activities and attributes identified here can serve as a diagnostic to help those involved in the process rate the importance of each role's responsibilities, as well as determine how effective individuals currently in these roles are delivering against those responsibilities.

Chapter 14: Reasons for Appointing a Non Executive Director

The Non Executive Director is the best kept secret of most successful companies; whether a temporary appointment or a full time fixture, the Non Executive Director contributes a wealth of knowledge, experience and contacts to the business.

A company does not have to be well established to be looking to bring a Non Executive Director onto their board. In fact it is strongly advisable for start-up companies and small and medium Enterprises (SMEs) to search for and recruit the perfect person to be a Non Executive Director for their organisation.

But why do you need one? Apart from having a great title and making your company appear soundly structured, the Non Executive Director has a lot to contribute. Providing they are carefully chosen, there are a great number of benefits to your company.

1. **Improved Board Conduct**

Many boards, regardless of how much training they have been through and how practised they are, can often fall into bad habits. Items are brought up which are not on the agenda, conversations are sidetracked, and day-to-day business is brought up. Introducing a Non Executive Director to your board meetings will encourage your chair to keep things on track. Time is important and the meeting needs to be specific and to the point.

The non-exec is usually a more experienced business person with a respected background which will also encourage other members to come to each meeting prepared and eager to both please and learn. This can be especially important in a start-up company where the ideas are great but needs direction and management. Sometimes a firm, but constructive, response from an experienced non-exec can ease any tensions.

2. They Have Seen It All Before

As previously mentioned the non-exec is an experienced business person who has probably helped a number of companies find their feet or survive through some tough times. There will not be many things that this person has not experienced and dealt with before. You can feel safe in the knowledge that, no matter how troubled you may be by an issue, your non-exec will have dealt with this issue before or know someone who has! They will be able to rationalise any worries and assist your board and managers in setting clear tasks to achieve what needs to be done.

3. It's Not Always What You Know

The most successful businesses are connected. Networking involves making great connections and keeping them. It can be a time consuming and difficult process to build up a trusted network of contacts that you can call on for expertise when you need them. Relationships take time to develop, and you just may not have that time to devote to networking. A Non Executive Director usually offers a diary of excellent contacts to go along with all their experience. Years in their chosen field has earned them the respect of their peers and fellow businessmen and businesswomen. If you need to make an important connection to help further your business, the non-exec will probably be able to make an introduction.

For start-ups this could mean connecting you with a supplier, distributor or potential client that could really boost your productivity or trading. For more established companies this could be a marketing guru or potential partner which would add new dimensions to your business, or make a change of direction.

4. They Look At The Big Picture

The Non Executive Director does not work with the company full time. They have no interest in the day to day running of the company but are there to focus on the Big Picture. What is the direction of the company? Are targets being met? Who is the growing competition, and what are the plans to keep ahead?

Often boards can get bogged down in the detail of some fairly insignificant day-to-day management and structure and lose track of the wider issues.

The non-exec will ensure that all board members are aware and acknowledging changes in the environment (economic, socio-political etc) and implementing strategy to deal with this. Having seen changes sweep over the business sector in the past they will be able to advise, with confidence, the direction they think it may go and how you can place yourselves to achieve success. You will be amazed at what they will notice that other board members may miss, and again how beneficial your Non Executive Director's contacts are at sounding an early alarm!

5. They Are Not Afraid To Be Honest

Because this expert does not work with you day to day, does not engage in office politics and retains their independence, they are able to offer unbiased, constructive criticism at all times. All boards try to behave as professionally as possible, but there are times when they are only told what they want to hear and very important lesson learning opportunities can be missed.

When you have a Non Executive Director casting their eye over the way the business is conducting its affairs, you can be assured they will ask probing and pertinent questions, in order to get to the real detail. They can ask the difficult questions because everyone understands that they are doing it purely for the good of the company and not for the benefit of a personal agenda within the company.

This does not mean that they will be constantly criticising, but rather encouraging the board to be accountable for decisions they have made, and praising them when they have achieved good work (even at times where it may not have gone to plan).

6. They Bring Out The Best

A good board is one with a broad range of personalities, strengths and experiences. Great talent and intuition can be lost or overpowered by stronger voices if it is not nurtured. A Non Executive Director will often spot those people whose potential isn't quite yet being fulfilled and offer advice and support in order to grow their confidence or efficiency. In small companies and start-ups it is not uncommon for a non-exec to work for a short time with the directors to help them identify their strengths and weaknesses and understand how they can work more effectively together by playing on those strengths.

You really don't need to take much more time considering whether your business needs a Non Executive Director. They are an incredibly valuable asset to any company, at any stage and you will quickly start to reap the benefits.

Chapter 15: The Personal Attributes of Effective Non Executive Directors

Non Executive Directors have four broad responsibilities to provide advice and direction to a company's management in the development and evaluation of its strategy; to monitor the company's management in strategy implementation and performance; to monitor the company's legal and ethical performance; and to monitor the veracity and adequacy of the financial and other company information provided to investors and other stakeholders. As part of their monitoring responsibilities over company management, NED directors are responsible for appointing, evaluating and where necessary removing senior management, and for succession planning for top management positions.

Clearly, effective NEDs need experience relevant to carrying out these broad responsibilities. Whether through prior experience or through training provided by the company or outside educational institutions, they also need adequate knowledge of the particular company on whose board they sit. But relevant experience and company-specific knowledge are not enough to make an effective NED.

According to the evidence collected by the Higgs Review and confirmed in the corporate governance overview, effective NEDs need four personal attributes to carry out the responsibilities of their role:
- Integrity and high ethical standards.
- Sound judgement.
- The ability and willingness to challenge and probe.
- Strong interpersonal skills.

There is no doubt that integrity and high ethical standards are essential for effective NEDs. But other qualities are required as well. NEDs must exercise sound judgement based on knowledge about the company and the environment in which it functions. They must be able to recognise problematic company actions or a flawed decision-making process. They must be able to identify issues of risk and judge how and when to raise them.

NEDs must be able and willing to challenge and probe the information presented to them by company management. According to a recent survey by AA Global Sourcing, companies cite the willingness to confront management and raise difficult issues as one of the most important characteristics of an effective
NED.

Strong interpersonal skills are essential. Without such skills, an individual NED will not be able to participate fully on a board of highly talented individuals or to question the recommendations of powerful executives. NEDs must have sufficient strength of character to seek and obtain full and satisfactory answers within the collegiate environment of the board.

In an analytical report prepared for the Higgs Review, Professors McNulty, Roberts and Stiles conclude that effective NEDs also need high levels of engagement and independence:

"Effectiveness requires high levels of engagement ... It is not sufficient just to turn up at board meetings. Instead individuals need to build their knowledge of the business through all sorts of informal contact with executives, as well as their work on board sub-committees. Only with this sort of engagement and understanding of a company can individuals make a credible contribution to board discussions." (McNulty, Roberts, Stiles, 2003)

NEDs need "independence of mind" that allows them to test and challenge executive thinking on the basis of their experiences elsewhere. In the words of the Higgs Review.

"A major contribution of the Non Executive Director is to bring wider experience and a fresh perspective to the boardroom; although they need to establish close relationships with the executives and be well-informed, all Non Executive Directors need to be independent of mind and willing and able to challenge, question, and speak up."

In addition, some NEDs must not only be independent thinkers, they must be independent in the stricter sense that there are no relationships or circumstances surrounding their involvement with the company that could affect or appear to affect their decisions as board members.

In summary, the model NED must have relevant experience and adequate company knowledge. He or she must also be honest, ethical, challenging, able to express his or her views candidly and convincingly, engaged, and independent of mind. Aviva Chairman, Pehr Gyllenhammar, suggests useful guidelines for the selection of NEDs with the phrase **"no crooks, no cronies, no cowards"**.

The Current Composition of Non Executive Directors

Many successful individuals from diverse backgrounds in both the commercial and non-commercial sectors have both relevant experience and the four personal attributes required to serve as effective Non Executive Directors. There is nothing to suggest that previous boardroom or top management experience is the only source of relevant experience required for effective NEDs. Nor is there anything to indicate that such experience is either necessary or sufficient to guarantee the four personal attributes required to carry out the broad responsibilities of NEDs. Yet the background surveys and research performed for the Higgs Review found that previous boardroom or top management experience is often the main, and sometimes the only, competence that companies seek from candidates.

Food for Thought

The Higgs Review found that the majority of NEDs in UK companies are white, middle-aged males of British origin with previous plc director experience. In the survey of companies completed for the Higgs Review, non-British nationals accounted for only 7% of NED positions, while British citizens from ethnic minority backgrounds accounted for only 1% of such positions. The survey also found that although about 30% of managers in the UK corporate sector are female, women hold only 6% of NED positions.

Chapter 16: Non Executive Directorship Best Kept Secret

It's assumed by many small business owners that NEDs are the things of big businesses or major corporations, but recruiting the right NED can help a small business gain experience, knowledge, contacts and ideas as well as constructive criticism; all of which cannot fail to be of value to a company regardless of its size.

So...what are the benefits of NEDs?

Got the t-shirt

NED can fill a gap in a small business owner's experience or can add industry knowledge of a specific sector the business is targeting. Whatever the reason a NED will be an experienced business person with a respected background who has probably helped a number of businesses find their feet, grow or survive tough times and, if a NED is faced with a situation they have never dealt with before, they will know someone who has.

Think outside the box

A NED doesn't work with a business full-time and won't be concerned with day-to-day issues but will instead look at the bigger picture. What is the direction of the business? Are targets being met? What environmental changes might affect the business? Which competitors to watch out for and what are the plans to keep ahead?

NED doesn't work with the business day to day, does not engage in office politics and retains their independence. In addition, a NED will have witnessed changes sweep over the business sector in the past. All of these factors mean they will have the ability to advice with confidence and make unbiased decisions in the interests of the business.

Connections that count

A successful business is a connected one and a great way of making connections is through networking. However, for a small business it can be time consuming and can often prove difficult to build a trusted network of contacts. NED, in many cases, can offer an address book of relevant contacts to go along with their own experience. This could be suppliers, distributors or potential customers to help boost business or a marketing guru or potential partner to add a new dimension to your business.

Keeps the management team in check

Many boards become the victims of bad habits; missed agenda items, conversations being side tracked, and opinions being discounted. The introduction of a NED will not only help to keep things on track but can help alleviate tensions and "put out fires". Time is important for small businesses and meetings need to be specific and to the point.

In fact NEDs can round off a board by not only providing experience and knowledge that other directors may not have, but by being able to take a more objective view of issues affecting the business and offering a wider sense of the possibilities for growth.

Chapter 17: UK Corporate Governance Code

This chapter is based on UK law as at 1st February 2010, unless otherwise stated. The UK Corporate Governance Code sets out its own view of the role of the executive board, the chairman and the Non Executive Directors.

The role of the executive board

The UK Corporate Governance Code sets out its own view of the role of the board. This can be summarised as:

1. Providing entrepreneurial leadership.
2. Setting strategy.
3. Ensuring the human and financial resources are available to achieve objectives.
4. Reviewing management performance.
5. Setting the company's values and standards.
6. Ensuring that obligations to shareholders and other stakeholders are understood and met.

The Code recognises that there are some issues that can only be decided by the board. It states that; "there should be a formal schedule of matters specifically reserved for its decision" and that the annual report should include a "high-level statement of which types of decisions are to be taken by the board and which are to be delegated to management".

The chairman

The chairman leads the board, sets its agenda and ensures it is an effective working group at the head of the company. He must promote a culture of openness and debate and is responsible for effective communication with shareholders. He must ensure that all board members receive accurate, timely and clear information.

The Code says the roles of chairman and chief executive should not be held by the same person.

"There should be a clear division of responsibilities at the head of the company between the running of the board and the executive responsibility for the running of the company's business. No one individual should have unfettered powers of decision".

The chairman may not always be a part-time Non Executive; many are full time and describe themselves as executive chairman, but the roles of chairman and CEO are at least distinct. In addition to the responsibilities described above, the chairman ensures there is a good working relationship between the executive and Non Executive Directors and sufficient time to discuss strategic issues.

By contrast, the chief executive has responsibility for the day to day management of the company and putting into effect the decisions and policies of the board.

Any big public company combining the roles of chairman and CEO will have to persuade shareholders that the right checks and balances are in place.

Equally to be frowned upon, according to the Code, is the previously widespread practice of a chief executive stepping up to become chairman of the same company. Those against the practice argue that a new chief executive is going to have a next to impossible job if his predecessor stays as chairman, constantly looking over his shoulder and perhaps disagreeing with any departure from past policies. Those in favour sing the praises of a chairman who may have years of experience with the company, still has much to offer and who is quite capable of establishing a good working relationship with a new CEO.

The Code does concede that in exceptional cases the rule may be broken. Any board in breach should consult major shareholders in advance and set out its reasons for the appointment, both at the time and in the next annual report. Banks, in particular, have argued that only the incumbent CEO has the knowledge and experience of a large, multinational group's operations to fulfil the chairman's role.

This view received some indirect backing from the Walker Report, which argued for a greater emphasis on relevant industry experience among Non Executive Directors. And much play was made of the fact that of the three UK banks that failed in 2007–2008, RBS, HBOS and Northern Rock, none had a chairman with a banking background. In contrast, the chairmen of HSBC and Standard Chartered, which emerged relatively unscathed from the banking crisis, were lifetime bankers (and both had stepped up from the chief executive role).

Case study: How Marks and Spencer got its way

Marks & Spencer is a rare case of a major company where the roles of chairman and chief executive have been combined.

In 2008, the chief executive, Sir Stuart Rose, was handed the chairman's job as well in contravention of principle A.2. Shareholders muttered that this was contrary to the Code, but the company stressed that the roles would be split again when Sir Stuart retired in 2011. In the meantime, the new chairman's dominance would be counterbalanced by the senior independent director, who was given special responsibility for governance issues.

When a resolution was tabled at the July 2009 AGM calling for the early appointment of an independent chairman, it received an unusually high level of support, from 38 per cent of voting shareholders, but 62 per cent backed the board, and Sir Stuart remained in place. Despite that, a new chief executive joined in early 2010, and the roles were once again separated.

The role of the Non Executive Director

The Code clearly gives a strong role to the Non Executives. Their job description includes:
1. Constructive challenge and help in developing proposals on strategy.
2. Scrutiny of management's performance in meeting agreed goals and objectives and the monitoring of performance reports.
3. Satisfying themselves on the integrity of financial information and that controls and risk management systems are robust and defensible.

4. Determining appropriate levels of remuneration for executive directors.
5. Appointing and removing executive directors, and succession planning.

The Walker Report has re-emphasised the constructive challenge part of the job, in the light of the perceived quiescence of bank directors faced by a dominant chief executive. And the role of the Non Executives in setting pay in banks has been widened beyond the executive directors to include firm-wide policy and particular oversight for the pay packages of the most highly paid non-board members.

The Non Executive Directors should convene regularly, as a body, with the chairman, but without their executive colleagues; and at least once a year they should meet on their own under the leadership of the senior independent director to appraise the chairman's performance.

If the executive directors have a collective interest in any matter that goes to the board, the Non Executives may effectively be left in control. This situation is commonly seen where a bid for the company is received from the management team, or from a private equity group with management involvement. The executives can play no part in the decision, and it will be for the independent directors to decide alone whether to recommend the bid to shareholders.

Walker also put a time commitment on the role in a major bank board; a minimum of 30 to 36 days a year for at least some of the Non Executives. The Code says that all directors must be able to allocate sufficient time to the company to perform their responsibilities effectively. Less time will be needed for smaller companies and those with less complex businesses, but, with a norm of 10 board meetings a year, additional committee meetings and off-site visits, the job should be no sinecure.

Independent Non Executive Directors

The Code makes a distinction between Non Executives who are independent and those who are not. To qualify for the former category, an individual must not only have the necessary independence of character and judgment but also be free of any connections that may lead to conflicts of interest.

The Code makes it clear that someone will not normally be considered independent if:

1. They have been an employee of the group within the previous five years.
2. They have a material business relationship with the company or have had one within the previous three years, including an indirect relationship as a partner, director, senior employee or shareholder of an adviser or major customer or supplier (this would catch a partner from, for example, the company's audit firm moving on to the board after retirement).
3. They receive remuneration from the company in addition to director's fees or they participate in the company's share option or performance-related pay schemes or they are members of the pension scheme.
4. They have close family ties with any of the company's advisers, directors or senior employees.
5. They hold cross-directorships or have significant links with other directors through involvement in other companies or bodies (this works against the old boys club method of appointing Non Executives: Eddie is finance

director at company A and sits as a Non Executive on the board of company B; Eric is chief executive at company B and sits as a Non Executive at company A).
6. They represent a significant shareholder.
7. They have served on the board for more than nine years.

Ultimately, however, it is up to the board to decide who "qualifies". The board is expected to consider the above and, indeed, any other factors that may impair independent judgment; but none of them is to be thought of as grounds for automatic "exclusion". It may be that an individual is judged to have the strength of character and integrity to remain unaffected by circumstances that, in theory, compromise their independence.

Sir David Walker, in his 2009 review of governance at major banks, argued for less emphasis to be placed on the independence of nonexecutive directors for the sake of it and for greater weight to be given to relevant financial industry experience. Independence in name was less important than "the quality of independence of mind and spirit, of character and judgment".

When they appoint Non Executives, and each year when reporting to shareholders, the members of the board have to identify who is independent and who is not. If they have decided that, despite previous and/or current connections with the company, etc, an individual may be classed as independent, they need to explain the reasons why.

Chapter 18: Non Executive Director Remuneration

The career of a Non Executive Director (NED) is rewarding, especially when a non exec director carves out for themselves a specialism around transactional environments where they are brought in to help groom the business for sale. Non Executive Director Pay, as such can vary massively between non exec appointments and ranges in various types of business. National Health Service (NHS) Non Executive Director pay may be vastly different to that of a NED working within a FTSE Listed business where Non Executive Director pay can reach £100,000. NHS Non Executive Director vacancies tend to be anything from £6,000 per annum to £25,000 per annum (depending on whether the organisation has achieved NHS Trust status).

In most Non Executive Director remuneration research, there is an obvious split between Non Exec pay in the top listed businesses and the smaller private companies and more-so in the non profit Non Executive Director roles which are vast (these include non NHS Non Executive Director vacancies). The differences can be remarkable but the top earners often must have very high profiles and this is not a career option open to most non execs.

According to the Institute of Director (IOD), typical Non Executive Director earnings are in the region of £6,000 to £25,000 per year in non listed or small businesses; a figure which is still handsome to many as most Non Executive Directors are expected to commit one day per month! In many cases, Non Executive Directors manage to enjoy full time permanent employment alongside one Non Executive Director role. The role of a Non Executive Director varied and day rates can be high.

Non Executive Director's compensation should consist solely of a cash retainer and equity-based compensation. The cornerstone of Non Executive Director compensation programmes should be alignment of interests through the attainment of significant equity holdings in the company meaningful to each individual director.

We believe that equity obtained with an individual's own capital provides the best alignment of interests with other shareholders. However, compensation plans can provide supplemental means of obtaining long-term equity holdings through equity compensation, long-term holding requirements and ownership requirements.

We believe that companies should have flexibility within certain broad policy parameters to design and implement non-executive director compensation plans that suit their unique circumstances. To support this flexibility, it argues that investors must have complete and clear disclosure of the philosophy behind the compensation plan, as well as the actual compensation awarded under the plan. Without full disclosure, it is increasingly difficult to earn investors confidence and support for compensation plans, including both non executive and executive director plans.

Although Non Executive Director compensation is generally immaterial to a company's bottom line and small compared to executive pay, we believe that Non Executive Director compensation is an important aspect of a company's governance; because director pay is set by the board and has inherent conflicts of interest, care must be taken to ensure there is no appearance of impropriety.

Chapter 19: Board Diversity

Question:
Why should my company care about whether the board of directors is diverse? And how do I, as a diversity practitioner, help make that happen?

Answer:
Board diversity has several benefits. It gives organizations new ideas and innovative solutions at the strategic level; it helps attain and retain the best talent; and it helps organizations market and protects the brand.

Most companies have a great deal of difficulty getting gender and racial/ethnic diversity on their boards, even though the talent pipeline from those groups is growing. While 60.4 percent of master's degrees went to women two years ago, according to the National Centre for Education Statistics, and more than 15 percent went to Blacks and Latinos, the Fortune 500 is very low in board diversity.

The U.S. Securities and Exchange Commission (SEC) Commissioner Luis Aguilar echoes the connection between board diversity and business results in an interview with Diversity Inc CEO Luke Visconti. Aguilar states that "companies with better performance seem to have more diverse boards." A new report by the Committee for Economic Development (CED) contends that giving women a seat at the table and providing adequate talent development not only can deliver measurable business gains but is the key differentiator in future global success.

Jim Turley, global chairman and CEO of Ernst & Young, No. 6 in the Diversity Inc Top 50, acknowledged the link between board diversity and company performance, stating: "We have focused on diversifying our board because we know it enables our firm to perform better."

With the best available talent, boards are more likely to identify and select diverse senior leadership. Diversity Inc Top 50 data also shows a positive correlation between diverse boards and diverse executive-management teams. According to the EEOC, national senior leadership in private industry is 11 percent Black, Latino and Asian and 28.2 percent women. In comparison, the Diversity Inc Top 50's senior leadership is 17.7 percent Black, Latino and Asian and 24.1 percent women. The Diversity Inc Top 10's executive management is even more diverse.

Diverse boards can ensure that contributions align with company and shareholder values related to diversity and inclusion. In "Are Political Donations That Conflict With Your Diversity Policy a Shareholder Issue?" North Star Asset Management's Julie Goodridge and Christine Jantz show how corporate political contributions that violate company values risk the company's good name and shareholder value.

Best Strategies to Diversify Your Board

Based on our data and sustainable results, we recommend the following approaches:
1. Mandate diverse slates for every board opening.
2. Do not look at the "usual suspects," those same women, Blacks, Latinos and Asians you see on so many corporate boards. Look down a level or two to people with great ideas who may be younger or have not yet achieved your "qualifications."

3. Maintain clear communications between the board and your chief diversity officer so everyone understands diversity strategies and priorities.

Chapter 20: Diversity the Canadian Way

The Canadian Board Diversity Council (CBDC) has created Canada's only national database of qualified, diverse candidates for corporate board of director appointments – Diversity 50. In two years, in collaboration with the 10 Diversity 50 CEOs/Chairs, they now have a database of 100 top, board-ready candidates for corporate board service.

Diversity 50 is designed to help corporate directors identify board-ready diverse candidates beyond their own networks. How do they define diversity? The Council's definition expands the traditional board definition of industry experience, management experience, functional area of expertise, education, geography and age to also include such considerations as ethnicity, gender and aboriginal status. The Diversity 50 database allows you to search 78 specific fields such as industry experience, functional area of expertise and gender to name a few. Like in any search for a new director, the onus remains on a board's nominating and governance committee (and their executive search firm) to exercise due diligence and assess the potential candidate's credentials against the board's requirements.

HSBC Canada President and CEO Paulo Maia, Deloitte Managing Partner and Chief Executive Frank Vettese and the eight other CEOs have developed and vetted the qualification criteria for Diversity 50 in collaboration with the Council. In turn, the Council collaborated with GMI Ratings, a leading independent provider of global corporate governance ratings and research with a database of over 130,000 public company directors.

It is important that corporate directors meet the Diversity 50 candidates in person. The Council was pleased to facilitate these introductions for its Members' boards of directors and executive teams at private receptions hosted by the select CEOs. The Receptions were held in Vancouver, Calgary, Toronto and Montréal in November 2012 and September/October 2013. The Council also piloted a Diversity 50 Reception with executive search firms in Toronto in June 2013.

They invite boards to join the Council and mitigate the risk to business of not having the diversity of thought and experience at the table to drive shareholder value.

The Council and Diversity 50

The Canadian Board Diversity Council (CBDC) is the leading Canadian organization advancing diversity on Canada's boards. The Council is self-funded thanks to a growing number of member organizations following initial funding from the federal government.

There vision is for Canadian companies to become more globally competitive in part because more boards are comprised of directors who are the most qualified in a greatly-expanded talent pool. In other words, imagine if Canada's boardrooms look like Canada! Canada's multicultural population provides a wealth of talent, connections and perspectives.

Are quotas the answer?

The Council does not support quotas at this time. Instead, they support a made-in-Canada approach. First, they advocate boards recruit beyond their own directors' networks. Through a rigorous process to identify new directors who are not known by the current directors with the assistance of search professionals and the Council through Diversity 50, boards can benefit from well-credentialed individuals who bring a wider range of skills, experiences and perspectives to corporate governance. This means better discussion, greater diligence in decision-making and ultimately, improved financial performance and shareholder value.

Second, made-in-Canada approach means the Council conducts annual research to track progress. They deliver a hard copy of the Annual Report Card to each FP500 director. In this way, directors can contextualize the composition of their own boards. Third, they provide the tools that member companies boards need in order to execute a board diversity strategy. Fourth, the Council created 'Get on Board', which provides a cost-effective orientation to board service. Fifth, they help member organizations be successful in the execution of their own diversity strategies.

Diversity 50 does not guarantee board seats for the candidates. Diversity 50 is intended to:
1. Motivate boards to embrace greater diversity by providing a pool of potential candidates who are not in board members' individual networks.
2. Motivate potential candidates to be more active in their searches. The Council advocates that boards follow a rigorous process to identify and recruit new directors in collaboration with search professionals.

Diversity 50 underscores the importance of boards identifying candidates from traditional and non-traditional pools and provides a forum for interested individuals to communicate their interest in corporate board service. It is up to the individual board (and search firm) to assess the individual's competencies against the board's requirements when conducting its due diligence during a search.

Chapter 21: NHS Non Executive Appointments and Ethnic Diversity

A truly representative NHS needs more diversity among trusts Non Executive Directors.

In June 2009, the Government Equalities Office and Cabinet Office set new targets and an action plan to increase diversity in public appointments - including NHS non-executives.

The document stated that "We are not doing this because it is the politically correct thing to do; we are doing it because there is a real value in having these different perspectives around the board table".

"These are important, paid roles responsible for the stewardship of billions of pounds of taxpayers' money, for services that touch people at their most vulnerable and for thousands of staff in their organisations. They should be open to as wide a range of people as possible so that boards can reflect the make-up of modern society".

As of late 2009, one of the targets has been achieved in the NHS. People from black and ethnic minorities account for just over 10 per cent of NHS non-executive directors. In part at least, that is down to the Appointments Commission, which is responsible for recruiting and appointing non-executives.

Commission chief executive Andrea Sutcliffe has adopted a strategy of attracting as wide a range of people as possible to apply for non-executive roles. For example, she has worked with the Progressive Muslims Forum both to identify high calibre candidates and uncover the barriers to them applying. More locally, she has worked with trusts and primary care trusts to identify places they might advertise vacancies to attract a broad range of candidates.

She insists the target has been achieved without any compromise on quality of appointments.

"We absolutely will continue to appoint on merit the best people to these jobs," she says.

"We are not doing this because it is the politically correct thing to do," she says, "we are doing it because there is a real value in having these different perspectives around the board table."

Delving Down

Although the figures look reasonable, she adds "If you delve down to local areas you do not necessarily get boards that reflect their local populations. Boards only have five non-executives so they are never going to represent every minority. We need to consider whether board members reflect and connect to the communities they serve."

The question is this; how do boards move beyond the tick box? How do they avoid the danger that the black and minority ethnic (BME) member is seen as the representative for all BME communities and uniquely qualified to chair the equalities committee?

"I think there is a crucial role for chairs here," says Ms Sutcliffe.

Ranjit Sondhi, chair of Heart of Birmingham Teaching PCT, and Naaz Coker, chair of St George's Healthcare Trust in London, would both agree. Ms Coker says: "The target should be the starting point, not the end point."

At St George's she set up a board level equality and human rights group that assesses all new services for their equality impact.

"I started it and used to chair it but now I have handed over to another board member - a female barrister. There is enough knowledge on the board now for me to do that," she says.

She is moving to a focus on equality. She says: "The agenda now is to focus on who we exclude and why."

Mr Sondhi, chair of Heart of Birmingham since 2002, points out that over 70 per cent of its population is classified BME - but even that fails to capture the richness of "super diversity".

"We have people from new communities that are not captured in the census, such as Yemeni and Somali," he says. "We have increasing numbers of people of mixed race. And then cutting through that are all the other categories of diversity, such as age, gender, sexual orientation and poverty."

A board cannot be representative of such complexity and anyway, he says: "Representativeness does not mean effectiveness and understanding."

But service delivery to such a diverse community depends on an awareness of what this means at board level.

"If it is not happening at board level, it will not happen at service delivery level," he says.

His approach has been to recruit a wide range of non-executives who are connected to their communities.

"We have had all sorts of people," he says. "Among the best were an 82 year old African Caribbean person and a Muslim bus driver."

He has filtered notions of diversity and equality with a board led induction programme for all PCT staff and beyond that focused on quality.

"We try to maintain the principle that we maintain the same high quality of service to everybody, regardless of their background."

The debate goes on!

Chapter 22: Women at the Top

Number of female executives at FTSE 100 companies is falling despite efforts to boost women in industry.

Two female conservative MPs called on major firms to publish detailed information on how many women they employ and to take fresh action to help female employees climb the corporate ladder.

Therese Coffey and Mary Macleod, who both worked in industry before being elected, said promoting women was not only fair but also made business sense.

In a report for the Conservative Women's Forum, they said the latest figures for women executives were "stark", with just three female chief executive officers heading FTSE 100 companies; Carolyn McCall at EasyJet, Angela Ahrendts at Burberry and Alison Cooper at Imperial Tobacco – compared with five two years ago.

Barely one executive director in 20 (5.8 per cent) is a woman, a fall from 6.6 per cent last year, while 15.3 per cent of positions filled by women in the tier below the board is lower today than six years ago.

The MPs said the falling ratios contrasted with increasing numbers of women in major companies worldwide. They warned: "The UK is slipping behind while competitors across the globe are making progress."

They urged companies to publish details of numbers of men and women at each level of management, how many employees are promoted by gender and the pay gap between the sexes.

Firms should offer mentoring programmes for women, as well as formalised schemes allowing for women who take career breaks to have children. Employers should also encourage part-time and flexible working, the MPs say.

They called on the Government to bring in plans for tax-free childcare vouchers next year rather than in 2015 and to improve careers advice for girls with a view to encouraging more to pursue science, technology and engineering subjects.

Ms Coffey said: "There is strong evidence that having more women in senior management improves a company's financial returns, corporate governance and decision-making. As women are the key consumers in society, businesses without executive women are losing their connection with their market. UK companies simply cannot afford not to make the most of their female talent."

A report for the Government by Lord Davies set out plans to increase the proportion of women on FTSE 100 company boards from 10.5 per cent in 2010 to 25 per cent by 2015. The ratio has now reached 17.3 per cent, but the MPs noted that the increase has not been replicated lower down the corporate hierarchy.

They called for him to be asked to turn his attention to appointments in the public sector and professional services and noted: "A man joining a top law firm is ten times more likely to make partner than a woman."!

New breed of female Non Executive Directors are helping to increase the number of women on FTSE boards.

"Non Executive roles are not for everybody," according to Ruby McGregor-Smith, the chief executive of FTSE 250 outsourcing firm Mitie. "A Non Executive role can be quite regulatory, it doesn't suit all people," she says.

The UK's first female Asian to run a FTSE 250 firm is talking about the go-to topic of the moment: how to get more women on boards and keep them there. Sure, there is been an increase in the number of women taking up Non Executive posts in the last few years, following a major push by some chairmen and the government to increase diversity at the top. But the glaring lack of women appointed to executive roles on those same boards is being swept under the carpet.

By increasing the number of women in non-exec roles, are we really solving the issue of a lack of diversity and a supposed lack of well-thought through decision making at the top? Or are we just playing a numbers game?

There has been a lot of discussion on women on boards recently, that is great, but women need to decide where they really want to be. Becoming a Non Executive Director might sound impressive, but as she points out, the job can be quite process-driven; it can be one of checking and monitoring rather than necessarily creating and being creative.

Of course, each NED role varies from company to company. But getting more women doing these roles doesn't solve overnight the current problem of Britain's biggest companies not utilising women's skills. If the majority of exec roles still go to men, then how much are companies really seeking fresh skills?

Becoming an NED is just one option in many that aspiring businesswomen can hanker after. Female entrepreneurs regularly tell me they hate the thought of sitting around a stuffy boardroom, trying to keep up with bags of paperwork and providing a second pair of eyes to something, when actually, they want to be in the hot seat themselves. This includes being in a start-ups.

Why are executive roles seemingly harder to get?

But if women want to make it to an executive FTSE role, they may find it harder. Research shows that even despite the recent awareness drive on the lack of women at the top, companies still tend to recruit exec posts based on financial experience; which men tend to have more of. Companies are less likely to take a chance giving an executive job to a woman without that experience, but they would take that chance on her for a part-time non-exec role.

As board sizes diminish partly in response to increasing accountability and improving corporate governance in wake of the financial crash there are simply fewer exec posts going, which makes it even harder for women to fill the few core, exec jobs going.

I would encourage career women to research both the industry and the type of role they think they might like to end up in future, to make sure it will be stimulating enough and utilise their skills. In industry today, there are plenty of opportunities for women (and men) to make their mark.

Equally the UK's growing start-up scene has been a great place for women to forge and own their careers.

Why would you choose to work in an industry that hasn't embraced flexible working and will hinder your path to the top? In other words, don't necessarily go for a job working in a company that has not regularly promoted women or simply got around the thorny issue of "women on boards" by recruiting more NEDs, but has made no effort to stimulate its own pipeline of female executive directors.

Most of all, young career women should stop this idea of trying to have everything at the same time; you can have it all but over your lifetime.

It's true that a bit of NED experience can lead to an executive job further down the line; but the two roles are actually quite difference, as we outline below.

Non Executive Directors

According to the Institute of Directors, Non Executive Directors are expected to focus on board matters and not stray into executive direction, thus providing an independent view of the company that is removed from day-to-day running. Non Executive Directors, then, are appointed to bring to the board:
1. Independence.
2. Impartiality.
3. Wide experience.
4. Special knowledge.
5. Personal qualities.

Chairmen and chief executives should use their nonexecutive directors to provide general counsel and a different perspective on matters of concern.

Non Executive posts are usually part-time roles and directors can have multiple roles at different companies on the go at once.

According to the Chartered Institute of Personnel and Development, Non Executive Directorships can offer lucrative recompense along with opportunities for broadening cross-sector exposure. However, the legal duties and responsibilities should not be underestimated, either by those considering such directorships or the companies seeking to appoint them.

It is recommended that within all listed public limited companies (except those below FTSE 350) at least half the board should comprise of Non Executive Directors.

Executive directors (often just called "directors")

Executive directors have a more hands-on role in designing, developing and pushing through strategic plans for the business. Typical roles include chief executive; finance director and IT director.

Company law dictates that a private company must have at least one director; a public company must have at least two directors.

Directors are responsible for the day-to-day management of the company. In smaller companies directors and shareholders may be the same people but the roles are very different and distinct. In the UK Directors are also governed by the Companies Act 2006 and are regulated by the registrar of companies at Companies House.

Chapter 23: General Perspective on Diversity

European Union (EU) backs move to boost numbers of female non-executive directors. Legislators back rules demanding firms to choose women when men are equally qualified; but stop short of quotas.

The European parliament has backed rules that would give women preference for non-executive posts at companies, after plans for a mandatory quota to get women into top jobs were scrapped.

The rules demand that companies give non-executive directorships to women where there is no male candidate who is better qualified, until they reach a target of four in 10 being women.

"The parliament has made the first cracks in the glass ceiling that continues to bar female talent from the top jobs," said EU justice commissioner Viviane Reding, who launched the proposal.

Although the draft law envisages possible fines for firms that ignore selection rules, it has been softened from imposing a quota with a penalty. Nor do the rules help women aiming for top management roles, such as chief executive. They also exempt smaller companies and those that are not listed.

Only about 17% of non-executive board members in the EU's largest companies are women. In Britain, women hold 17.4% percent of directorships, up from 12.5% in 2010; only three CEOs at FTSE 100 companies are women; this is a number that change all the time.

If endorsed, the rules will take seven years to come into full force. Countries are now required to sign off on the law but are divided on whether Pan-European rules on positive discrimination are necessary.

Britain and Germany have argued against mandatory quotas.

Men dominate boardrooms in the region, and many women who have risen through company ranks resent quotas because they can be seen as suggesting that women have not been promoted on merit.

Only Norway, which is not a member of the bloc, has enforced a 40% quota since 2009, although critics say this has been achieved in part thanks to a small number of women holding non-executive positions in multiple companies.

Collectively, women and minorities lost ground in America's corporate boardrooms between 2004 and 2010, according to Missing Pieces: Women and Minorities on Fortune 500 Boards 2010 Alliance for Board Diversity Census. Six years after the first ABD Census, this report shows that white men still overwhelmingly dominate corporate boards with few overall gains for minorities and a significant loss of seats for African-American men. In the Fortune 100, between 2004 and 2010, white men increased their presence, adding 32 corporate board seats, while African-American men lost 42, and women particularly minority women did not see an appreciable increase in their share of board seats. In the Fortune 500, which is included in this year's report as well, the overwhelming majority of seats were held by white men.

The study was compiled by the Alliance for Board Diversity (ABD), a collaboration of five leading organizations Catalyst, The Executive Leadership Council (ELC), the Hispanic Association on Corporate Responsibility (HACR), Leadership Education for Asian Pacifics, Inc. (LEAP), and The Prout Group, Inc.

"With so many qualified women and minority candidates available for board service, it is staggering to find that no real progress has been made in the past six years to advance minorities and women into the boardroom," said Ilene H. Lang, Chair of ABD and President and CEO of Catalyst. "Research has shown that diverse teams produce better results. In particular, Catalyst research revealed that more diverse boards, on average, are linked with better financial performance. Corporate America has the opportunity to seize the advantage that a more diverse board can yield in this increasingly competitive global economy."

Key findings from this report include:

In the Fortune 100, between 2004 and 2010:
1. Men still dominated boardrooms. In 2010 they held 82.0 percent of board seats; in 2004, 83.1 percent.
2. White men have actually increased their share of board seats in corporate America from 71.2 to 72.9 percent. Minorities and women shared the remainder, with very few seats occupied by Asian Pacific Islanders, Hispanics, or minority women in particular. With the exception of African-American men, who lost seats, the percentages have not changed notably since 2004.
3. More specifically, African-American women held 2.1 percent of seats; Hispanic women held 0.9 percent; Asian Pacific Islander women held 0.5 percent; African-

American men held 4.2 percent; Hispanic men held 3.1 percent; and Asian Pacific Islander men held 1.7 percent.
4. Although women gained 16 board seats; 7 occupied by minority women the overall 1.1 percentage point increase over 6 years was not appreciable.

In 2010, the ABD expanded its research to include companies in the Fortune 500. Fortune 500 boards were less diverse than Fortune 100 boards.

Men held close to 85 percent of all board seats. White men dominated the board room, holding 77.6 percent of board seats. Minority men held 6.8 percent. White women held 12.7 percent. Minority women held 3.0 percent. More specifically, African-American women held 1.9 percent of Fortune 500 board seats; Hispanic women held 0.7 percent; Asian Pacific Islander women held 0.3 percent; African-American men held 2.7 percent; Hispanic men held 2.3 percent; and Asian Pacific Islander men held 1.8 percent.

Approximately one-half of Fortune 500 company boards were composed of 20 percent or fewer women and/or minorities. Women and minorities were significantly underrepresented in Fortune 500 board leadership positions. White men held 94.9 percent of board chair positions. There was not a single Latina lead director or board chair.

In 2010, 15 companies achieved broad board diversity: each of the major U.S. Census groups was represented in their boardrooms.

We still have a long way to go to achieve diversity in the board room!

Chapter 24: Conclusion

A Non-Executive Director (non-exec) is a part-time role as opposed to the normal full-time directors of a company. They normally bring skills, contacts and guidance to businesses. Although part-time they are legally as much directors of the company as the full-time ones. They will not however have anyone reporting to them and will not generally be involved in the day-to-day running of the business.

Traditionally it has been the larger company or PLC that has had non-executive directors and a major part of their job comprised corporate governance. However, more lately, smaller companies and even start-up businesses have taken on non-execs to fill out their management team with experienced and well connected business people.

Non-execs are part of the management team, therefore not the same as consultants or even mentors, however just like consultants and mentors, they will bring benefits in terms of their knowledge and experience.
1. Non-execs can provide expertise that you normally could not afford to buy.
2. They are more committed than consultants or professional advisors.
3. Adds credibility to the management team (especially helpful to gain funding).
4. May have contacts that would assist with obtaining sales or in understanding the market.
5. May purchase shares in the business, or have access to funding sources.
6. Will be a sounding boarding for the MD or CEO.

7. Brings years of experience to bear when looking at proposed business plans.
8. Can provide crucial guidance at critical stages of a business.
9. Fill particular skill gaps which the owners or founders of a young company may not have.

Often non-execs will also have a full-time job, or have more than one non-exec role, as long as it's not a competitor this is good, because it is this outside knowledge and contacts that you will find valuable. Generally you should expect them to be present at monthly management meetings and on a few other days during the year, on average say 18 - 20 days. The actual time is entirely up to yourselves to agree.

Non-execs pay is negotiable and there are quite a few permutations available. Some are paid by the day, some may have bought or been given shares in the business that attract dividends and some may have an annual retainer. The amount will vary depending on whether you are a large PLC or a start-up. A 2006 survey from the Institute of Directors (IOD) found that for those working in larger companies the average pay per day was £2,080, and for medium size companies it was £867. For small businesses it could be less and for start-ups it may solely be shares in the business that get earned over a period of time.

As an example, one privately owned medium size company (approx £1m Turnover) gave a 1 or 2 percent share of the business to each of two non-execs (the full-time directors/founders owned the rest), based on this they paid the non-execs a share dividend equating to about £400 a month. This paid for the non-execs time and ensured they had a keen interest in the company.

For many non-execs it isn't just about earning money however, these are people who have made their mark already and may be looking to encourage and help aspiring young businesses to achieve. They may be happy with just a small monthly retainer, or welcome the ability to purchase or earn shares in an exciting opportunity.

Your perfect non-exec may already be known to you. For smaller companies it may be someone you worked with in the past, or a client that already knows the business sector and has good industry contacts. There may be a well-known or prestigious person in your industry that you could confidentially approach. You have to consider what it is that you are looking to achieve.

The insights and advice of those who have contributed to this book has been invaluable. When asked what would be the most important piece of advice they would wish to impart to an individual taking on a new Non Executive role, the following observations were made...

1. Be prepared for the unknown.
2. Take time to build your relationships.
3. Trust your instincts; first impressions are usually spot on.
4. Don't think you need to make a contribution from day one; take time to understand the key issues and don't jump to early conclusions.
5. Don't short-cut the due diligence once you join, it can be hard to leave.
6. Be really clear why you are doing this and why it is of benefit to you; what value do you bring and what experience will you gain? Make sure it's a win-win.
7. Think about your Non Executive role as a logical building block that builds on the experience you have

and enables you to shape and influence your career as you wish.
8. Get feedback from your Chairman after your first year and ask yourself if you are really adding value.
9. Don't be afraid to put your head above the parapet to ask the awkward question.
10. Be absolutely certain you trust the Executives.
11. Ensure you focus on the key issues.
12. Make sure the culture is right; it drives everything.
13. Initially focus on listening and understanding rather than contributing.
14. Understand the character and relationships of the others on the board not their caricatures.
15. Have humility and don't take yourself too seriously.
16. Make sure of your facts before opening your mouth. There will be a moment when you don't agree with something. If it is about the way an action is being implemented; keep quiet and don't teach the Executives to suck eggs. If it is about the decision to do something, speak out.
17. Is it a company you are interested in and can be passionate about?
18. Be respectful of the company and go with the flow of the business.

It is a great privilege to be in someone else's boardroom. A Non Executive Director occupies a special place to influence rather than provide direction.

Good Luck!!

Printed in Great Britain
by Amazon.co.uk, Ltd.,
Marston Gate.